UNVEILING

This book is set in the typeface *Athelas* designed by Veronika Burian and Jose Scaglione.

Unveiling is a publication of Taj62 Media LLC.

Memoir collaboration and development by Nicholas Poe.

Paperback ISBN: 978-1-967262-10-6
Hardcover ISBN: 978-1-967262-11-3

Produced in Partnership with *Tall Pine Books*
PO Box 42 Warsaw | Indiana 46581
www.tallpinebooks.com

| 1 25 25 20 16 02 |

Published in the United States of America

UN
VEIL
ING

A Memoir

MY LIFE JOURNEY FROM *VEIL* TO *VISION*

SAHAR SAEED

Dedications

In memory of my loving and kind father—You taught me so much in the fleeting time we had together. I carry you with me in every step I take, in every word I write, in the woman I have become. Your love, wisdom, and legacy continue to live on—not only through these pages but also through my life. Your regarded influence still resonates, inspiring many, just as you always inspired me.

To my heroic and resilient Jewish family, my brothers and sisters—You have taught me to fight—with courage, perseverance, and unwavering love for God. I deeply admire your strength and your steadfast faith. Thank you for standing in the gap and fighting on our behalf. May we never cease to pray for you and remain faithful in supporting you—not just in words, but in action and truth.

To my brothers and sisters in Christ who come from Muslim families—You have had the courage to swim against the current, silencing every voice but one—the voice of Truth. Congratulations! I know the weight of your journey, the pain of walking away from everything familiar—your family, traditions, heritage, and friendships. I know the cost is high, but your reward is far greater.

Our God is faithful. He is a rewarder of those who seek Him, and He finishes what He starts. May this book be a source of encouragement, reminding you that transformation is possible and that you are never alone.

Endorsements

"Guided by dreams, visions, and the Spirit of the Lord, Sahar's journey is truly an adventure. It reflects a simple yet profound desire to bridge divides and reveals how a love for the Jewish people naturally flows from a salvation experience where Christ reigns and His word leads. If I tried to capture her best insights, I'd probably have to write a book of my own. For Jewish believers, it's a deeply moving sight to see someone from so far away step into our world and walk away having encountered God on an even deeper level. Without a doubt, God is doing something remarkable in Sahar's life. I pray God continues to use her to break down the dividing wall."

—ALEXANDER BLAIR

COO, *Swords Into Plowshares*

Gainesville, FL.

"Through this insightful memoir, you'll come to experience how God, in His mercy, directs our steps across faiths, generations, and continents. If God can use Saeed, the youngest daughter of a large Shia Muslim family in an ancient Saudi city, transform her heart for Christ, and use her to be His voice at the global intersection of Abrahamic faiths, what might He do through you?"

—KAREN BEJJANI

Author of *The Blue Cord,* CoFounder of *iHOPE Ministries*

"An unforgettable memoir of courage and awakening, *Unveiling* is Sahar Saeed's radiant journey from devotion through doubt to defiant faith. With lyrical storytelling and searing honesty, she challenges the narratives that bound her and invites us into a new vision of reconciliation and hope. This is a bold, necessary voice for our times."

—NASSER AL-QAHTANI
Founder of *The River of Life Network*
Middle East/North Africa

"Sahar's captivating life story draws back the curtain on a relatively unknown world for many American believers. Each chapter reveals challenges Muslims face as they are drawn to Yeshua. Readers will be spurred on to live out the Great Commission with Arabs in their community. Get ready to be challenged to live as a true brother/sister of Jesus Christ, like Sahar: counting the cost, then doing exactly what the Father in heaven wants (Mark 3)."

—ANONYMOUS ENDORSER
Eastern Province, Saudi Arabia

"*Unveiling* is a prophetic voice and a courageous invitation to freedom. Sahar's journey from the veil to radiance is a powerful call to every Saudi woman—and beyond—who is searching for worth, identity, and the true beauty found only in Christ. Her story unveils the inner conflict of seeking truth and the divine revolution of love, redemption, and revealed identity that only God can birth within the human soul. With grace and eloquence, she gives voice to a rising movement of healing and hope. In a time when the world so desperately needs bridge-builders, not wall-makers, Sahar stands as an ambassador of reconciliation and peace."

—NIZAR ELAIMY
Founder and Director of *Joy TV*
Nazareth, Israel

"In an extremely polarized world, Sahar's captivating testimony forges a path of love, unity, and courage. This book is exactly what our world needs, especially the Middle East: a fresh worldview that boldly defies animosity, political and religious hatred; it is a beacon of hope for a new day in the Middle East. Read it with an open heart, especially if you have former conclusions, education, or experiences. This is your invitation to be part of the solution our generation is longing for! From Arabia to America, Israel and Palestine, Sahar's unique journey weaves together cultures and storylines in an intriguing, beautiful tale you won't be able to put down!"

—SARAH GERLOFF
Jerusalem, Israel

Contents

From Veil to Vision

This is my story. In *Unveiling*, I recount my raw, unfiltered journey from veiled obedience to a bold life of vision, freedom, and reconciliation. It's not just about what was removed—but what was revealed: a calling to rise above history and build bridges that heal.

Setting the Stage

I never imagined my journey would lead me here—standing in the midst of what many would call an *impossible* reconciliation.

Being born into a devout Shia family in the heart of Saudi Arabia, from my very first breath, I was taught that Shia Islam was the only true path to God. Christians, Jews, secularists, and even Sunni Muslims all had it wrong. Our way was the right way.

I was taught that God does not have children, and that the Bible's message was nothing more than a corrupted version of God's true word. I was told that Christians no longer followed the true path, and their Gospel was a shadow of its former self—distorted, broken, lost. I was also told that Jews were the enemies of God because of their disobedience. I heard the Quran's harsh words, describing Jews as being "like a donkey that carries a load of books but does not benefit from them." I was taught that Israel was an oppressor—a nation that had no right to exist, especially in the heart of the Middle East. This wasn't just political; it was *personal*. These teachings became my identity. They shaped my understanding of the world, my faith, and my place within it. Questioning these beliefs was unthinkable, even treacherous.

My quest for answers took me across the globe to the United States, where I came to study. What I found there challenged everything. I didn't just earn a degree—I encountered something that would shatter the walls I'd built around my heart.

Through time, I've visited Israel and had a first-hand experience of Tel Aviv's vibrant energy, walked Jerusalem's sacred streets, and stood in Nazareth, where Christ's message first echoed. I fell in love with Israel's story, its culture, and its people. I now fight for a future where unity crushes the bonds of hatred. I made a choice—to stand with Israel, no matter the cost.

In time, I saw Israel through the eyes of faith and hope, not conflict and fear. I saw Israel for what it truly was—not an oppressor, but a miracle. A nation reborn from the ashes, a people who had survived against all odds, standing as a testimony to God's faithfulness.

Choosing this truth came at a price.

But I stand today for something bigger than myself. Something that cannot be ignored. I refuse to accept the lie that Arabs and Jews are doomed to live in conflict. I refuse to be shackled by the chains of history's divisions. I believe we are called to something greater—to a shared destiny where we rise together, where hatred gives way to understanding, and where we build a future not of division, but of unity.

This is why I have committed to being part of a movement dedicated to transforming enemies into partners, fear into trust, and division into collaboration. Inspired by the Abraham Accords, I see the hand of God at work—helping to heal a rift that has lasted for millennia. A plan of reconciliation unfolding right before our eyes.

This book is not just my story; it is a clarion call to all who are ready to question the narratives we've inherited. To rise up and embrace a destiny of peace, not war. To choose love over hatred, truth over lies, and courage over fear.

I refuse to wait for change.

I am the change.

This is our moment. Our mission. Our time to write a new chapter.

Let's rewrite the story—together.

CHAPTER ONE

An Early Hero

My First Love

"She did not stand alone, but what stood behind her, the most potent moral force in her life, was the love of her father."

—HARPER LEE

I was outside the boundaries but right where I belonged. Sitting comfortably, I giggled as a trespasser in my own childhood home. It was quite easy for a five-year-old girl in the Middle East to find restrictions and forbidden places. I was no exception. Our property sat along a quiet street surrounded by sand and other sun-dried brick homes. Inside our doors, a cool rush of air offered relief from the arid heat of the desert. We had the predictable features of any home. The foyer led to a kitchen with a dining area, bedrooms, and bathrooms. Unique to our culture, however, was the presence of *two* living rooms or "Al-majlis| المجلس".

These dual living spaces were not a display of wealth or a symbol of luxury. Instead, they served a very practical purpose: to separate men from women, boys from girls. This segregated socializing was not just a cultural norm but an Islamic obligation. Men would have Arabic coffee from small *finjan* cups | فنجان while arguing over how to solve the world's problems. Properly separated, women would then be able to remove their coverings for conversations of their own. If guests were over, only after proper notice was given could a man enter a female space.

The border I had crossed into male territory on this particular day was one that I had crossed many times before. Conventional Saudi Arabian etiquette would call for repercussions or consequences for such an action. For me, however, there were none. In fact, my unlawful entry was welcomed—celebrated, even. I had a special open invitation from my father, who valued time with me more than cultural rules. Being the baby girl of four daughters, I had carved out a unique little throne for myself in my dad's heart. This gave me unprecedented access.

I recall sitting in his lap, playing with his beard, and listening while he talked with male relatives, friends, and colleagues. My dad had built a career for himself in the oil industry and worked in the business complex by the waters of the Persian Gulf (Arabian Gulf). He was employed by one of the largest oil companies in the world and had climbed his way up the corporate ladder through the years. In fact, this job was the very reason we were situated in Al-Khafji, an industrial city on the Arabian coast between Kuwait and Qatar.

A career in oil meant we encountered an array of nationalities who visited Saudi Arabia from around the world. From a young age, I was exposed to diverse Middle Eastern cultures like Palestinian, Syrian, Lebanese, Iraqi, Egyptian, and Kuwaiti people. Beyond that, many Westerners also worked with my father, Europeans and Americans alike. In that precious forbidden space, I recall hearing English accents and seeing unique Western clothing devoid of the usual male *thawb*[1] | ثوب and *ghoutra*[2] | غترة. It felt like a little international hub right there in our home.

At the time, I did not realize that my father was giving me a much-needed glimpse of broader societies and cultures. In that living room, he created a small world for me with diverse backgrounds, languages, people, and experiences to observe. This served as a type and shadow of a life to come, where the Father would also build a world for me full of diverse experiences and pursuits abroad. With his blessing, my dad enabled me to do what I should not have been able to do in that day. Likewise, a time was coming when I would find myself in places I would normally not be permitted to carry out tasks that would usually never be assigned to me. My time in the male living room was not

1. A long-sleeved ankle-length traditional robe mainly worn by men.
2. This is a broad cloth folded and held in place by a camel's hair cord known as an 'iqāl.

just playtime—it was a prophecy.

In a small way, my dad was giving me a taste of doing the impossible.

This should come as no surprise, considering he had essentially done the impossible himself. Coming from a dysfunctional family full of turmoil and difficulty, my dad was not born with a golden spoon in his mouth. His father, my grandfather, was a lawyer, a liar, and a playboy—not exactly the ideal resume for a man in the ultra-conservative Muslim world. He was always in trouble with other women while married to my grandmother, which ultimately led to their divorce when my father was still a teenager.

Under the patriarchal system, my grandfather had no legal obligation to pay alimony or child support of any kind. Of course, he did neither and abandoned his family altogether. This left my father, the firstborn son, to care for his mother and younger siblings. He was forced to grow up overnight. Being responsible for the household meant finding work, and finding work meant getting involved in oil. He worked hard to provide for his mother, two younger brothers, and a little sister. Serving them with all of his heart, he put food on the table and eventually provided for their education and even paid for their weddings.

Essentially, he was a father before he ever became a father. He picked up the responsibility that his own dad had sadly dropped. Many men become hardened or cold under such circumstances. My dad was not like "many men," though. He was different in every way and drew upon a private source of strength. He was defying the odds and making the most of the brokenness he was left with.

While he navigated his newfound responsibilities, my mother was coming of age in her household. Also born in Al-Qatif, her parents knew my father's family well. Her dad was a truly good man with a solid reputation locally. Her mother, on the other hand, was a shadowy figure. She was not relational—which is an understatement—and tended to hide herself from others. Even as a child, I recall feeling no warmth from my grandmother. Her face was misshapen with dark eyes and a strange flat nose. As a small child, I inquired, "Why is her nose like that?"

"A demon in the house came and changed her face," I was told.

It was an unsettling revelation, to say the least. She and my grandfather had several children together, and then, after a substantial break, my mother was born. Some of her older siblings were already marrying and having kids of their own when she and her little brother came onto the scene. Her childhood was anything but normal. In fact, it was cut short altogether. At the tender age of 12, she was engaged to be married to my father. Initially, he came with his parents accompanying him to ask for my aunt's hand in marriage, but she was already engaged by that point.

"You have a younger daughter?" they followed up, "Is she available?"

At first, the answer was a hard *no*. Most people in that community at the time were married very young, generally between the ages of 17 and 20. Twelve was unreasonable, so my mother's dad offered a compromise.

"You can marry her, but you must be engaged for two full years first. At 14, she can marry."

The drop-on-one-knee, Western, Hollywood-style engagements were nowhere to be found in the patriarchal Middle East at the time. Historically, in many Eastern cultures, arranged marriages were the standard mode of operation. The parents of the groom-to-be would initiate a meeting with the parents of the potential bride and negotiate the engagement. Couples did not date, and the first time they would even lay eyes on each other was usually at their engagement.

The concept of marriage was abstract for my mother, as it is for most young girls. Because Saudi public schools are segregated by gender, she had never had friendships with boys, nor did she understand how to relate to them. With a very religious Shia family, this segregation was strictly enforced. The engagement came as quite a shock. When my father, her new fiancé, visited to spend time with her, she was understandably shy. In fact, she recalls playing, staying occupied, and giving her soon-to-be husband no attention whatsoever. Furthermore, to avoid being in the room alone with him, she would bring in one of her cousins to sit with them.

She felt awkward and unsettled. When my dad would say, "I love you," or when he would write letters to her, she lacked any good response. She had no relational tools to relate to a man outside of her family, let alone a fiancé. Like a quickly draining hourglass, her childhood days were numbered. She was going the way of so many young Middle Eastern girls. Her destiny had been arranged, and matrimony was unstoppable. As she began her teenage years, and as my father began his twenties, their wedding was slated to occur with conventional Middle Eastern flair.

* * *

Al-Qatif is an ancient coastal city, nestled within the Eastern Province of Saudi Arabia, also known as Al-Khut | الخط. To the northwest sit Kuwait and Iraq, and to the southeast Bahrain and Qatar. This particular city is one of the oldest in the entire Middle East, having been continually inhabited for over 3,500 years. For centuries, pearl divers have swum the depths of the Persian Gulf (Arabian Gulf) surrounding the city. Today, wooden fishing boats still gently sway in the warm water, having brought the day's catch to the oldest fish market in the Arabian Peninsula. The corniche, a paved walkway along the edge of the water, is bordered by palm trees. Their shade relieves families picnicking on blankets in the grass, enjoying the fresh, salty air, and taking pictures of the coastline with their phones. Like a timeless magnet, ancient and modern families alike have been drawn to these gorgeous waters.

Al-Qatif, meaning *the harvest*, consists of a coastline and a land mass in the water called Tarout Island. The city has a reputation as an oasis town, with natural springs creating rich soil that supports green foliage. Lush palm trees grow inland alongside dates, figs, and pomegranate trees. A refuge from the desert heat, the sprawling homes are spacious with living rooms bordered with soft carpets and embroidered floor sofas and pillows that invite guests to sit and stay a while. Every side table has a bounty of dates, nuts, and fresh fruit. The soft hum of the air conditioning, the chatter of extended family and friends coming to visit, and the pouring of fresh coffee are familiar sounds on long afternoons.

Within a small apartment in this city, in 1979, my mother and father were married. At that time, the family, friends, and neighbors would all gather in a flat area at the top of a house. Prior to the wedding taking place, the engagement | الخطوبة would occur with an Imam or Sheik who would come to the house to officiate the signing of a marriage license in the presence of at least two witnesses[3].

---

3. The engagement concept in Islam is actually quite similar to the Jewish custom: in fact, we even use the same word: Al-Khitbah (الخطوبة). Technically, the couple is considered legally bound during this time, but they are still getting to know each other while preparing and planning for the wedding day. In both Islamic and Jewish traditions, the engagement phase is more than just a promise: it's a legal and spiritual commitment. In Islam, Al-Khitbah (الخطوبة) often includes a formal gathering and, in many cultures, a signed agreement that makes the engagement official. Similarly, in Judaism, there is Erusin (אירוסין), the first phase of marriage, which also involves

The wedding itself was not a twenty-minute ceremony followed by a two-hour reception as is the Western custom. Instead, it was a full three-day ongoing celebration. The first day would involve henna tattoos for the bride, where her hands would be embellished with intricate designs, inviting blessing and favor. The second day would incorporate dancing, food, and traditional Arabic clothing.

At the close of their ceremony, my parents left the oasis of Al-Qatif, our family's homeland, to settle in Al-Khafji, where I would be born. My father had just been hired at a major oil company, and the newlyweds would travel a few hours up the coast to start their lives together. Despite her youthful hesitations, my mother's feelings grew for my father, and they fell in love as they built a life together. Their marriage was happy and sweet, a welcome contrast to the many marriages at the time that were poisoned by misogyny and even abuse.

My father took excellent care of his wife, loving her deeply and treating her as his equal. So much so that her friends, who often had unhappy marriages, saw his behavior and were quite jealous of my mother. To this day, she speaks of him with the utmost regard. In more ways than one, he seemed to be pushing back against the standard Islamic traditions for life and relationships. He was throwing off the suffocating norms of the Middle East and pioneer-

---

a formal document, often a Ketubah (כתובה)—carrying legal and religious weight under Jewish law.

ing a life that was vibrant and free. One day, I would understand exactly why.

* * *

As the 1980s began, new possibilities were booming for the nation of Saudi Arabia. The government had just completed a buyout from the USA. Saudi college students, for the first time, began traveling outside of the kingdom for education, and digital technology was being emphasized at a governmental level. With a history of primitive tribal warfare and poverty behind it, Saudi Arabia was now emerging as a major economic player on the world's stage. It was a season of newness and possibility.

On the home front, my parents were experiencing a season of newness and possibility as well. It was shortly after their wedding when my mom became pregnant. The young couple was filled with a flurry of excitement, anticipation, and wonder. What followed was the birth of my oldest sister in 1981. Like a chain reaction, another girl was born in 1982, with yet another girl in 1983, and finally, *me,* the fourth, in 1984. We had quickly outnumbered my father, and he loved every minute of it.

While Dad worked, my mother had her hands full raising us. She brought us up to memorize passages from the Quran and always insisted on maintaining proper posture. Good posture came easily as I had been holding my head up on my own nearly from day one. I was described as having "thick bones," which made me a sturdy child, but a difficult one to birth.

I'm told my father saw something unique in me, nearly immediately, when I arrived. Just three weeks later, my mom saw something unique as well. She recalled the full story to me later in life. "You are special," she said, "When you were a few weeks old, I picked you up and your face was shining like a very bright light. I was terrified! I ran out of the room in fear...but I knew there was something special about you." She considered it to be a divine encounter of some sort but had not pieced together the *how* or the *why*.

Despite this short-term glowing countenance, I was a normal, peaceful child who enjoyed the simple pleasures of being a kid. As a family, we routinely had meals together, usually something like rice and meat, and some salad with zaatar bread. Being the youngest, I would forgo a chair and opt to sit on the dining table instead. I liked being up on that stage, and I savored the attention that came with it.

What did playtime look like for a young girl in Saudi Arabia? Usually running around in the sand, animating my dolls, and daydreaming. I spent much time outside, a place where my imagination had no ceiling. There was freedom in the outdoors with hot sand underfoot and a blue sky overhead. I recall giving my older sister a clothing design for my doll, and she would get to work stitching it. Dressed in young Sahar's latest fashion brand, the dolls would sip tea, gossip, and argue.

Next door lived an Egyptian family who had originally left Egypt and settled in Saudi for a better life. There were three daughters with whom my sisters and I played. To our right lived neighbors of the Bedouin variety who had a small herd of animals outside of their house. These sorts of neighbors were normal in Al-Khafji but completely *abnormal* in our family's original home city of Al-Qatif. While we did not raise herds of animals, we seemed to always have little critters around the house. Rabbits, cats, kittens, or colorful baby chicks that my father would bring home.

On the weekends, we would drive three and a half hours south to visit our family in Al-Qatif, and I began to notice the differences between the two cities very early on. Al-Qatif, for example, was a monoculture where all of the residents were very conservative Shia Muslims. Al-Khafji, on the other hand, exposed me to Sunni Muslims and non-Muslims as well. Women in Al-Qatif wore full niqabs, veils that covered everything except the eyes, whereas those in Al-Khafji wore hijabs, which exposed most of the face. While I appreciated the time with family, I relished the diverse nature of where we lived in Al-Khafji.

Spotting differences and making comparisons is an important developmental milestone for children. Existing between two very different cities facilitated this growth for me early on. I did not just exist between two cities, however, but two *people*. I was quite young when I took note of the stark differences between my mother and father. She was devout and read theological books on the Muslim faith regularly, which was unique for a woman at the time. Her strict adherence to that set of standards informed her parenting. This meant she lacked emotional availability and tended to favor superficial things like appearance and academics. In fact, the two maids at our house took care of me for the most part while my dad was at work. In truth, there was no intimacy with my mother. She was there, but not present. She lived in the house, but was not *alive* in the house.

At times, the days wore on and felt oppressive to my young mind. Limitations, shouts, and occasional smacks to the face became the hallmarks of interactions with my mother. I stole chocolates while she napped and questioned rules at every turn. The sweetest sound that always broke me from any spell was the noise of the garage door opening at about 5 pm every day.

Dad was home.

My mother's strict structure would be upended, and fun could be had again. Laughs and giggles that had been suppressed all day would now fill the air. When he walked in, he brought an atmosphere with him. The tyranny of my day would come to an end, and freedom could begin. My sisters and I had absolute permission to be *crazy*. He let us be ourselves through and through—never attempting to change or modify us.

"Don't mess up the bed," my mom would say as we jumped and threw pillows.

"It's ok, I'll fix it," my dad would shoot back in defense.

Thus, the jumping and mess-making continued with the blessing of Dad. My mom was quite a good cook, and we ate well and healthily. This meant I was often denied sugary desserts like *rahash* | رهش, which was a sweet, thick paste that could be eaten by the spoonful. I remember on one occasion being annoyed by my mom and then turning to my father, "Dad, I want some rahash." Unlike my mother's quick "no," he would stop everything to get me the treat.

I felt honored, cared for, and *seen*. With a little sassiness, I would eat slowly, making sure my mom was aware of every last bite. I had my way. Looking back, it's clear that what my mother attempted to shut down my father would encourage. In the mind of my father, things like messes, chaos, and disorder had their rightful place in the home as long as kids could be kids. His childlike joy and love were so authentic that one could not tell that he had been given such a difficult start in life. He not only worked through his family challenges, but worked through physical ones as well. He had a rare ailment of the kidneys called Buerger Disease (داء بورغر), which was exacerbated by long-term smoking— smoking that was a method of stress relief due to his plight. This led to the amputation of both of his legs before I was born. His prosthetics attached at the knee, and a cane assisted him wherever he went.

This physical limitation did not stop him, though. His outsized personality made him a beloved figure locally. He was funny and did spot-on impersonations of others, mirroring how they spoke and talked. He was well-respected and simply had no enemies to speak of.

As kids, we never questioned our standing with him. We were loved truly, completely, and without reservations. His hug was my safe place. He called me beautiful and funny and encouraged my young intellect. As he worked his way up in his career and began rubbing shoulders with international colleagues, Aramco provided him with English classes. Wanting the same opportunities for us, he would bring home English books and study guides that I would devour for weeks on end.

My curiosity about the world around me was exploding. In between running, playing, and singing, I occupied my time by asking an endless number of questions. From the moment I could talk, I had questions. *Who made the moon? Where does the sun go at night? How high can birds fly? Why is the ocean salty? Who put the salt in there?* I inquired about anything and everything. The books in the house fueled my imagination and creativity. My dad kindled the inquisitive fire in me and answered all of my questions, never once dismissing me or telling me to stop. He stewarded and expanded my mind. To this day, I feel I would die if I stopped learning.

From my dad, I learned to be generous with my time and attention. He welcomed all kinds of people to come to the house and eat with us, always sharing and giving money to those in need. He modeled a care and tenderness that I could find nowhere else. With him in my life, I was 100%, certifiably spoiled.

While approaching school age, however, my time as the baby was coming to a close. As my mom's tummy grew, so did my impatience. "When is he coming out? I want him to come out!" I would declare. My mom expected me to be jealous of this new baby, but I was actually enthralled. I was five years old when my sweet younger brother was born. Completely overjoyed, I quickly became a miniature mom, constantly wanting to watch him, touch his hands, care for him, and hold him.

While he was the firstborn baby boy, he would not be the last.

* * *

We gazed at the stars overhead, and I heard my father say, "The God who made those stars can be your friend." Even then, I recognized this as a curious way to describe God. It was not something I ever heard in the standard Muslim teachings. My dad had a knack for thinking beyond borders and ideologies, which certainly rubbed off on me. He conveyed a *personal* aspect to a relationship with God that Islam simply did not make available. He never prayed the Islamic prayers, and at night, he would lay hands on us girls and quietly pray over us before bed—something that Muslims simply did *not* do. The peace imparted during these times of prayer was tangible and undeniable.

On one occasion, he brought home a picture from work. How he obtained it, I'm still not sure. Nevertheless, to my mother's dismay, it was a drawing of Mary holding baby Jesus.

"This is Christian," she said, "why do we have this?"

"You believe He is a prophet. It's Jesus. I want it here in the kids' bedroom," he replied.

He placed it on the wall in the girls' room. It appeared so holy, ethereal, and beautiful. Who was this child? Why was He significant? Why does Dad want Him here with us? The wheels in my mind would spin.

Not only was my dad's prayer life and understanding of God unique, but he also understood Scriptural figures that other Muslims did not. For instance, he would always talk about the story of Job—the suffering man. Job's story was told in the Quran but with fewer details. My dad would recount Job's journey with insights that are *only* recorded in the Hebrew Bible. Clearly, he was dabbling in studies that broke the Muslim mold.

During that phase of life, he would need the example of Job, as those sufferings would become his own. The fight for his health had been long and tiresome, but it was not over. Now the fight was even more consequential, as he had a family who needed him. With four girls, one boy, and another baby boy on the way, my dad's health took a turn for the worse.

CHAPTER TWO

Deep Pain

Where did he go?

"What we have once enjoyed we can never lose. All that we love deeply becomes part of us."

—Helen Keller

The human experience on earth has a strange duality: the beauty of life and the tragedy of death can dwell so closely together. Sickness may destroy a man while ornate April flowers bloom just outside his room. The precious cry of a newborn is heard in the hospital while an aging grandmother passes away down the hall. A judge officiates a wedding in the morning and presides over a divorce in the afternoon. Joys and devastations both coexist in this life and force us all, without partiality, to navigate them. As a small child, Islam failed to provide me with a proper template for dealing with highs and lows, yet I was soon to encounter each.

When my baby brother was just learning to walk and talk, my parents brought another baby boy into this beautiful, broken world. As my new infant brother was carried out of the hospital to begin his life, my father was wheeled into the hospital to conclude his. The joy, newness, cries, and hope of a new child were met with the reality of my father's worsening health.

For months, he had been in and out of the hospital undergoing an array of treatments, none of which seemed to work. I recall riding in the car as a family on the roads that bordered the Persian Gulf (Arabian Gulf), with Dad at the wheel. He would playfully act as though he were driving us into the ocean, jerking the wheel and pretending to panic—a gesture that made us children shriek and laugh.

"Uh-oh, what if we all drown?" he would say.

We knew this to be a funny and light-hearted prank, though in hindsight, I can almost sense a subtle, underlying sincerity in this game. My father knew he was going to depart this life, and part of him wanted us to go with him, to reach the finish line together as a family. It was a fantasy he could toy with as we drove, but not an idea he could or would ever realize. As the car rolled along, with all our might, we sang the song we had recently made up.

"My father, Saeed, has the heart of a lion,

He will live, he will live, he will live!"[4]

---

4. Translated: Abuya saeed, qlb el asad ابوي سعيد قلب الاسد Yaeesh yaeesh yaeesh يعيش يعيش يعيش

My father did have the heart of a lion, and he did live on, just not in the way we expected. In his final days, he could not manage to speak, though he tried. He would write notes to communicate. His pain was immense, yet he looked at us children with passion while he lay on the hospital bed. We did what we could, which was to offer the last of the hugs and kisses we had to give him, along with our tears. I learned from my dad to talk to God about anything and everything, so I did much praying in private—*Please heal him, please don't let him die.*

My brother, who was two years old at the time, still retains a final memory of my father. He was being hugged while my dad wept and squeezed, knowing he would not live to see this little boy become a man. The crying frightened my little brother, and my uncle took him out of the room shortly after. Leaving behind four daughters, two sons, and a wife, my thirty-six-year-old father left this world and went to the place where he was finally free.

"Your dad died," a cousin informed me bluntly.

Being just seven years of age, I could only think of death in the abstract. *What does it mean?* I wondered. *Does this mean I won't see him any longer?* Shortly after his passing, women came to the house wearing all black and weeping. My heart was crushed, but the notion of death was not something I could fully comprehend.

When someone dies in the Islamic tradition, the manner in which people grieve is quite different than a Western, Christian arrangement, for example. Death is feared, dreaded, and no comfort or peace is to be found in the event. There is no assurance of salvation or hope of ever being reunited in the Muslim tradition. There is a finality and a defeat in death which I can only describe as Satanic. I looked around the house and saw women mourning, my mother was hitting herself, and my uncles were tearful yet stolid. Women would utter good things about my late father between sobs and cries. Amongst my siblings, I saw the common theme of confusion.

In the days ahead, we gathered for the funeral where there would be reading from the Quran and ritualistic prayers offered up, pleading with Allah to permit the deceased into Jannah[5] | الجنة. The attire would be dark, the mood would be grim, as men and women, properly segregated, took their sides within the husayniyya[6] | الحسينية. My cousins and I remained outside to play in the sand.

My tears seemed to be frozen and would not thaw for many years. I could not cry or laugh. I felt like a part of me died with my dad. I observed the events around me with a certain numbness that I could not manage to shake. I had no safe place to cry, process, question, or grieve. Neither my mother nor my relatives offered any sort of support, and I found myself going to sleep alone each night and without comfort.

---

5. The final abode of the righteous in Islam, or heaven.
6. A congregation hall for Shia Muslims where commemoration ceremonies occur.

I would talk to God, inquiring, *Where is my dad?* All I knew was that my hero had been taken from me, and I was now left in the hands of those who would not love me like he did. In the weeks and months to come, I would have dreams at night of my dad showing up at the house. He wore a shiny white outfit, bright and glowing with a sort of white that was not known in this world. He would say nothing but simply observe.

I found myself frustrated by his silence but delighted that he was present. He was in a better place now, and God was making that fact more and more real to me. The dreams felt so authentic and vivid that, at times, I woke up convinced that he was still alive and that I could walk into the next room and find him sitting there, inviting me to his lap. While that would not happen in this life, I knew deep down that he was fully alive and living on. Time would prove that those dreams were more than the imagination of a wounded child, but the communication of a loving God.

* * *

During the final stretch of my dad's sickness, we had moved from the diverse city of Al-Khafji back to our family's homeland of Al-Qatif. My uncle from my dad's side would give my dad a room to stay in while we bunked at my grandparents' house. Being back in Al-Qatif meant we were with our own people again—minorities in our nation but majorities in our city. See, before Saudi Arabia became a nation in 1932, it was just "Arabia" and did not exist as a unified country. Instead, it was a loose group of tribes that fought, conquered, and settled. It was known as an exile for troublemakers, rebels, misfits, and prisoners. Eventually, tribes formed, and the heads of those tribes would take on one another, blood was shed, alliances were formed, and power was grabbed.

Then came a man named Abdulaziz Ibn Saud | عبد العزيز بن آل سعود. He was a visionary leader who began an effort to unify the Arabian Peninsula in 1902 with the capture of Riyadh, his ancestral home, from the rival Rashidi dynasty. Over the next three decades, through a combination of military conquests, tribal alliances, and political marriages, he consolidated control over most of the Arabian Peninsula. His final major conquest was the capture of the Hejaz region in 1925, which included the cities of Mecca and Medina. It was one thing to take command of another tribe, but to unify an entire region and eventually, a nation, was something new altogether.

Thus, in 1932, having brought nearly a million square miles under his control, Ibn Saud put the "Saud" in "Arabia" and formally established the Kingdom of Saudi Arabia, proclaiming himself as its first king. There have been six leaders since. My tribe in Al-Qatif was originally from Iraq, Iran, and Bahrain, the majority of whom are Shia Muslims. The problem is, most Muslims in Saudi Arabia were and are Sunni Muslims, making my people a religious and cultural minority. After the Kingdom was set up, our people had been given the option to leave and return to Bahrain, Iraq, or Iran. Yet with roots deep in the region by then, many (my family included) stayed and lived as Shia in a nation built for Sunnis.

While I won't offer you a deep theological treatise on the differences between Shia and Sunni Muslims, I will give you a brief glimpse. In short, Sunnis believe that when Muhhamad died, his disciples and friends were to continue to expand his message. Whereas we, as Shia, believed that Muhhamad's family line and descendants should continue to push the message. In other words, Shia have fidelity to Muhhamad's lineage, whereas Sunnis maintain fidelity to Muhammad's message. While we all believed in the Quran, we interpreted it very differently. Looking back, I can see that Shia is a sort of cult within Islam, whereas Sunnis at least teach what Muhhamad taught, as wrong as it might be. Shia Muslims are to Sunni Muslims what Jehovah's Witnesses are to Christianity.

At just seven years old, I started to become aware of the differences we had with others throughout the nation. To say, "I am from Qatif," is to say "I am Shia." Al-Qatif was not just a popular city for Shia Muslims, in the way that Utah is a popular place for Mormons. Al-Qatif was *exclusively* for those of the Shia sect.

Because government officials and ruling religious leaders are Sunni Muslims who follow a strict flavor of Islam (often known as Wahhabism), my Shia people often faced severe persecution within Saudi Arabia. We were the marginalization weirdos of Saudi society with a history of martyrdom. We faced discrimination in the workplace and schools, as we are easily identifiable by our surnames and dialects. Nevertheless, my ancestors stayed and settled.

In the heart of this Shia region sat the home of my grandparents on my mother's side. Communal living and care for relatives are at the core of Saudi culture, and so my grandfather took us in following the death of my dad. It was an adjustment, to say the least. Just three weeks after the passing of my father, my grandmother died as well. It was sorrow upon sorrow in the home as we worked to find a new normal.

My twenty-six-year-old mother was now slated to raise six kids as a widow in a patriarchal society, which meant having her father's house available was a crucial help. Beyond the much-needed help with our living situation, when my father died, half of his salary came to us in a pension, *and* we had health insurance through the company in perpetuity. Uncles and relatives stepped up and generously gave help. An aunt on my father's side brought us things like gifts, clothes, watches, and money each month. Eventually, to my dismay, our mother put an end to it and pridefully rejected the help of anyone who came with a gift—treating them harshly so that they would not return.

On the other hand, my grandfather on my dad's side did

the opposite of offering to help. When my dad was alive, he constantly asked my father for money. Once he passed away, he tried to swoop in and take what he could from his late son. He took my dad's car and even asked for his wallet—not as a memento but as a last-minute cash grab.

My uncle took him to court to have him sign off and agree that he would lay no claim to my dad's money that was left to us. It worked out in the end. We occupied the middle to upper-middle class and lacked nothing growing up. Granted, we had classmates in school with parents who had government positions and connections, which meant they had seemingly unlimited money.

In Saudi, the rich either have a stake in the oil business or they have wasta[7]| واسطة. A person in Saudi Arabia could fail to graduate from high school, but if they had the right connections, they would climb the ranks higher in government than a person who only had credentials. Of course, every nation has a certain amount of corruption and nepotism, but it was particularly egregious in Saudi Arabia at the time. While it still exists, the government has worked to weed this out and now requires that you have both connections *and* qualifications.

I became keenly aware of this and other societal constructs as I began school. I saw the treatment of women in our culture and the lack of liberty as a whole. I witnessed

---

7.   A slang term in Saudi Arabia meaning "connections" or nepotism.

oppressive schooling where creativity was hushed and dreams were dismissed. I saw the vitriol for those outside of Islam, and I felt the suffocating life that was ahead of me. Yet there I stood, in silent opposition to it all.

* * *

The only time boys and girls are mixed together in a Saudi classroom is in pre-school, which I attended at the standard age of five. From there, we would not be separated by sitting on opposite sides of the room. We would not be divided into different classrooms within the same school. No, we would be separated by gender into entirely different schools altogether, with male teachers at the boys' school and female teachers at the girls' school.

While Shia Muslims were allowed to be teachers, they were not allowed to be in administration or teachers of Islam. Beyond that, they were forced to teach Sunni religion when on the job. To combat Sunni influence in school, my mother would teach us proper Shia religion at home. "It's wrong of the Sunni people to say that Abu Bakr was the first leader of the Caliphate," she would tell us. And we knew, even from a young age, that Imam Ali had been the first rightful leader.

My mother had a penchant for learning and often read theological books, at a time when reading of this kind was unusual for anyone in Saudi, especially for a woman. At home, we knew that we were Shia to the core, even though we acted as though we were Sunni in public, and despite adhering to a Sunni lesson plan at school.

Our classrooms were large, tidy, and quite nice. Ornate tile made up the floor, and we sat at sturdy individual desks. At the head of the room was a sizable chalkboard board and next to the chalkboard was a strict and ruthless teacher, whom a student must hold in high regard. We eventually dressed in gray uniforms and were expected to maintain orderly conduct. Should we step out of line or act up, our hands were abruptly slapped with a long wooden ruler. There was no dialogue to be had with teachers, and we were never permitted to share our minds or question the material.

As beautiful as the schools and buildings might have been, much of it was purely superficial. Behind the beautiful architecture was a decaying school system with ill-equipped teachers and poor methods for learning. The material written for young girls differed from the education of young boys. With the boys, they had a heavier emphasis on things like physics and chemistry, gearing them up to be the next generation of engineers, doctors, leaders, and mathematicians. After all, the father of Algebra, Muhammad ibn Musa al-Khwarizmi, was from this part of the world. As girls, our instruction may have included such things, however, the overall thrust in our education was pushing us toward one goal: becoming a wife and mother. While boys played sports, girls chose between three options: drawing, cooking, or sewing.

Early on, I found myself at the top of my class and thoroughly bored. Having three older sisters and an insatiable curiosity, I had already studied and memorized most of the material in the years prior. I was a natural learner and ate up the content. From Arabic to grammar to our six classes on Islam, I found school to be easy—too easy. When I realized I had fully grasped the topics at hand, I found my time in school from 8 am to 2 pm to be like prison daily.

I began to daydream. I longed to run, dance, and jump. Rigid boundaries just didn't sit right with me. I wasn't a rebel without a cause; I was wired differently. I had a wild imagination, an untamed intellect, and the educational system in Saudi Arabia didn't nurture my talents. I wanted to do anything but sit at a desk and stare at a board. This early battle with boredom created resilience, forcing me to develop strength and fierce independence early on—forging an unbreakable spirit and self-reliance.

Once, my mother was asked, "How is Sahar as a student?"

"She is smart and an excellent student...but she can't sit still," she added.

I cannot deny that description. I resorted to passing notes and making jokes in class. I figured if the school would not entertain me, I would entertain myself. Now and then, I found myself kicked out of class for laughing or causing distractions. On multiple occasions, I allowed my friends to cheat off my finished papers. This worked well for a while, until a friend copied absolutely everything on my English test word for word—including my own name! At that point, the jig was up.

The only other student who joined me at the top of a class was my best friend (Ebtihal | إبتهال), who was originally from Bahrain. We competed in our grades and bonded over everything else. Outside of my siblings and cousins, she was the one friend whom I spent the most time around. After school, we would go to her house where we would study and do homework, which was punctuated by a delicious meal from her mother, who was a wonderful cook. Her father, who was kind, loving, and truly interested in us, reminded me of my own. In fact, the atmosphere of the place was a comfortable haven and would put me in remembrance of our home in Al-Khafji before we moved.

In the big and the small, things were so different now in Al-Qatif. It was not just a new city but a new atmosphere and family culture as well. I recall saying to my mother, "My clothes are getting smaller."

"No, you are just getting bigger," she assured me.

This got me thinking about growth and what it meant. I followed up, "Can I mark my height on the wall to track how I grow?"

"No," she snapped. "We don't want to mark up the walls."

End of discussion. I cannot help but think that if I had

asked this of my father, he would have been the first one to rush to find a pen. "Great idea!" he might say, while picking a spot on the wall. With a soft smile, he would have balanced the pen on top of my head, marking a line and adding the date. He might have swelled with joy as he watched those little lines go up and up and up over the months and years as his little girl grew.

I was eternally curious and an idea machine. To this day, ideation remains one of my higher strengths, but at the time, no one but my father knew how to foster it. With him gone, I was left alone to see my gifts and curiosities doused. I secretly began marking the wall in a discreet location behind the fridge because I simply *had* to have data available on my growth.

As I worked my way through my early elementary school years, I realized I did not just have a hunger to learn but a desire to teach. I longed to export knowledge as much as I wanted to import it. Even as a young child, I would open books with a red pen in hand, pretending to grade the papers of my students. I saw what was lacking in the classroom at school and longed to one day bring about change. I thought I could one day connect with my students, to cater their education to them individually, and to discover the best modalities for their learning.

At the time, teachers were minimally invested, not highly educated, and the job itself lacked prestige. In a Saudi household dominated by pride, my mother was adamantly against my career prospects from the start. "You will *not* teach. You will be a doctor," she would say, and I would play along for the time being.

* * *

The monotony of long, oppressive days in school might be broken up with occasional childhood vacations to Bahrain—places where movie theaters were legal and life looked just different enough to be interesting. On the weekends, we did what all Saudi women do, which is pass the days at the mall—shopping, walking, buying clothes, browsing cosmetics, and talking. The malls in Saudi Arabia are not like any other. They're luxurious and gigantic. They act not just as a show of wealth but as community hubs.

Saudi women are the number one consumers of beauty products in the world[8] with Hong Kong being a distant second. I suppose this is what happens when women have nothing to do but stay home and look good.

The mall was always refreshing. With endless stores, sprawling play areas for children, and nice food courts, it was a one-stop solution for passing a Saturday. When not at the mall, we might be found at one of the several food markets in the area or at a local restaurant, some of which

---

8. Maceda, Cleofe. "UAE, Saudi Women Are World's Biggest Spenders on Beauty Products - Report." Zawya, July 15, 2020. https://www.zawya.com/en/business/uae-saudi-women-are-worlds-biggest-spenders-on-beauty-products-report-olmw8j0w.

were designated for men only. The family restaurants were outfitted with a curtain that separated each individual family from the others.

At that time, we didn't have many international foods in Saudi Arabia. You might find an Indian place or a Lebanese restaurant here and there, along with a couple of fast food options. Now, though, Saudi has everything that America would have, Chuck E. Cheese included. Children in Saudi Arabia today do not know the Saudi Arabia that I knew, and for that I am happy.

I was coming of age in a land that was far from westernized and still very fundamentalist. Two years after my father had passed, my uncles, who lived with us, would express aggravation at my not being covered. *You ought to be covered,* they would declare. Of course, I knew the day was coming when I would begin to live behind a black veil in public. Nearly all the women I knew did. I just didn't know it would be so soon.

So it was, starting at the age of nine, I was abruptly forbidden to play with my male cousins. New attire was given to me, and I was covered entirely, from head to toe, in black. From then on, I would only see the world through a small window in the veil.

CHAPTER THREE

Wrong Rites

A Look at Islamic Theology

"Well-behaved women seldom make history."
—LAUREL THATCHER ULRICH

The same dreams continued. I would see my father enter the home and look around, glowing yet saying nothing. Exasperated, I finally went to my mother to inquire, "Where is my dad?" I demanded to know.

"He died," she would explain. "God chose him to depart."

This, of course, made me angry with God, and I took it upon myself to inform him of my frustration.

"Hey, do you hear me, God? I'm here. Is my dad with you? Tell me." Failing to hear an audible voice, I then set forth a challenge to God, "If you wake me up at 9 am tomorrow, then I know you heard me and my dad is with you."

I went to sleep, and at exactly 9 am, I awoke, not to the

loud ring of an alarm but to a gentle tap on my shoulder. This was not the hand of my mother or a sibling. It was a very soft touch, and upon opening my eyes, I found that no one was at my bedside. In a flash, I recalled my prayer from the night before. I leapt up energized, excited, full of spiritual zeal, and ran to share the personal encounter with my mother.

"Mom, I told God to wake me up at 9 am and He did!"

"How dare you think you can talk to God like that?"

As you might imagine, my excitement was crushed. Quickly, she took me by the collar and walked me to my uncle, explaining to him my outrageous experiment. In a strict tone, he informed me, "That's not how you talk to God. He is not your *little friend*. Let me teach you how to pray."

He took me aside with his explanations. By his instruction, I learned that prayers were not available on the tip of the tongue, ready to leap from the heart, like my father had taught me. Instead, a rite called *wudu* | وضوء or *ablution* came before prayers might be uttered.

We began with the washing of the face. From there, one washes the lower arms from the elbows to the wrists, leaving no part dry. I was told to first wash my right arm with my left hand three times. Then my left arm with my right hand three times. With the remaining moisture on my hands, I wiped my head and then feet from toes to ankles. It was explained to me that the order must be absolutely perfect. If you make a minor mistake or get the chronology wrong in the slightest way, you must start wudu over from the beginning.

Once the washing is complete, one may recite the *du'a* اللَّهُمَّ بَيِّضْ وَجْهِي يَوْمَ تَسْوَدُّ فِيهِ الْوُجُوهُ وَ | دعاء. Which roughly translates, "لَا تُسَوِّدْ وَجْهِي يَوْمَ تَبْيَضُّ فِيهِ الْوُجُوهُ . اللَّهُمَّ أَعْطِنِي كِتَابِي بِيَمِينِي وَ الْخُلْدَ فِي الْجِنَانِ بِيَسَارِي وَ حَاسِبْنِي حِسَاباً يَسِيراً ." "Lord, make my face white the day faces go black, and don't allow my face to be black the day faces go white. O God, Grant me the eternal record of my life to be in my right hand, the affirmation of immortality in Paradise in my left, and moreover, grant me easy reckoning."

The purification ritual did not have its intended effect. I felt anything but pure. I found that hovering over the Islamic approach to God was a cloud of shame and guilt mixed with chronic uncertainty. I gathered that God was a cold, vicious dictator on the throne whose mood cannot be predicted or apprehended. He made heaven and earth, set up some rules, and then kept his distance. No, God is not a friend, nor is he a father like the Christians taught. Bibles, of course, were not allowed in Saudi Arabia, and what we knew about Christianity was a mere caricature of their faith. "Christians teach that God had a sexual relationship with Mary. They also worship multiple gods. Infidels," they would say.

We, on the other hand, had the full and total truth about God. Allah had made his final remarks in the Quran, and that was that. We did our best in the here and now while hoping to avoid hell in the hereafter. Things like assurance and certainty are pipe dreams in Islam. In fact, it is insecurity itself that propels us to devotion, not love or affection.

In truth, the day I learned to pray the Islamic way was the day that my freedom in God was killed. The peace, joy, and love I felt at my 9 am wake-up call were now gone, just a brief piece of history, and I would not rediscover it for another 18 years.

* * *

The days and weeks and months and years passed at my grandfather's home. It differed from what I had known before, both in appearance and culture. He had an open concept house with large rooms in a very old neighborhood nestled within Al-Qatif. On the floor were carpets and cushions with geometric patterns and floral motifs. Uncles would linger and debate on their own, while my mother would sleep late—sometimes well into the afternoon. This left me to feed, care for, and entertain my younger brothers. My grandfather slowed down with age, my sisters eventually began marrying, and the tension with my mother increased. To me, it was home, but it was not the home I once knew, nor the home I hoped to know in the future.

When the sun dipped below the horizon, winter winds would blow at night like cool whispers across the dunes. At daybreak, the sun blazed down on the endless stretches of sand, painting the desert in a myriad of golds and ambers. In temperatures that often reached 120° Fahrenheit, I would put on my garb and escape the chaos of my grandfather's house and walk to the bakala | البقالة with friends. Bakalas were small kiosk-like stores with basic necessities and snacks, found all over Saudi Arabia. Think New York City bodegas or a common 7-Eleven.

I always seemed to have money. Friends and I would bear the heat to go buy candy, chips, or drinks. We would visit the bigger markets—air filled with the aroma of spices and fresh bread, or we would pass the time at the sprawling malls. In those days, it was quite common to be approached by men before reaching the mall's entrance. In a near whisper, they would say, "Hey, here's 500 riyal, let me come in with you."

According to Saudi law, women could enter the mall by themselves without issue. However, the government did not allow men to enter alone, fearing they would go in to flirt with women. Allowing this, of course, would be the collapse of prudish Saudi life. This separation is cultural, but it's cultural because it's theological. Islam teaches against the mixture of men and women, espousing that a female is to preserve her beauty for her husband only. They felt that a mixture of genders could result in promiscuity. So, men who did not have a family would wait outside of the mall and bribe women for entry—and it usually worked.

What did these men proceed to do after getting in? Flirt with women, of course. With the mall being the only place to mingle, it wasn't uncommon to come home with a stack of telephone numbers from very direct men. It was the Middle Eastern way—eliminating any guesswork about intentions.

In the food court, my friends and I navigated the new challenge of eating in public as fully covered young ladies. Lifting my veil with each bite, I would carefully maneuver the fork under my niqab to eat.

I hated it. Every second of it. Everyone has a face. *What is there to hide?*

From there, I would make my way home, the sound of laughter with friends fading along the way. Behind my veil, I would subdue a smile as I neared my grandfather's house. Much laughing, according to Islam, is *fahisha*, meaning lewd and indecent. Allah was not a fan of joyful people, after all; true reverence for him cannot coexist alongside jokes and giggles. سورة القصص " لا تَفْرَحْ إِنَّ اللَّهَ لا يُحِبُّ الْفَرِحِينَ " "Do not exult; Allah does not love the Joyful ones" (Sura 28:76 AL-QASAS).

I entered childhood a free spirit and exited childhood a bound one. More than anything, I longed to be *free*—whatever that meant. Under my father's hand, I was me. With him gone, I was someone else. Prior to the move, I found myself easily excited, always anticipating both the big and small joys of life. Any outing was an adventure, and a new book was a planet to explore. When I moved to my grandfather's, I lost my sense of adventure—or more accurately, it was taken from me. The game had changed, and I was now sentenced to living like a good, Middle Eastern adult.

This was the suffocating rhythm of my young teenage life.

Beyond the mundane oppression of existence, I soon realized I was also living with demons. Creating a sketch of my grandfather's house would not be fully accurate without describing these demons, and no, I do not mean that in a figurative sense, and no, that's not a nickname for members of my family. I mean, I quite literally became acquainted with demonic activity while dwelling in the house of my grandfather. This was not cause to be concerned, however. My mother assured me that we had "good demons" in our midst, but I was terrified nonetheless. She recalled routinely seeing the waters in her childhood pool stirring aggressively when no one had been near it for hours. For me, I remember loud clacking coming from the keyboard of my computer despite no one being near it. Doors would open and footsteps could be heard, with no person around to cause the noise.

Misery, like an omnipresent shadow, lingered everywhere I looked. This was particularly true among women. From the Quran permitting men to strike their wives, to needless coverings, it felt as though women were dead seeds, pushed deep into the dirty soil with no chance at ever blooming or seeing light. Even then, I felt stirrings deep within my heart to help women, but I had no power to do anything about it. I was a mere spectator of the unfolding sorrow. I wrestled with the thoughts of elevating the lives of women while remaining anchored in the Islamic tenets. After all, Islam was not just a family identity but a substantial portion of our daily routine. We prayed once in the morning, had two prayers combined in the afternoon, and two prayers combined at night—or the equivalent of five scripted prayers daily.

Somehow, though, I believed deep inside the recesses of my heart that God was better than what I saw in the book. I couldn't help but feel he was more accessible than the rituals and rites would make me believe. I had the sense that prayer was more than a religious charade, and time would prove that right.

* * *

As a developing teen, I sought entertainment, spectacle, and fun. With movie theaters being illegal, we could only attend a show when in Bahrain. Fortunately for us, the Saudi government pre-approved certain television programs from Kuwait and Egypt, so we could enjoy some entertainment without leaving the house. They were generally dramas, dominated by plotlines of love, betrayal, or fights over money. They weren't great, but they were something.

As the show would begin, introduction music would play, and as the show ended, music would fade in during the credits as well. It was always at this point when our uncles, overhearing the tune, would shout from the other room, "Turn it off! Mute the music!"

Music was haram[9] | حرام according to Islamic tradition. The thought was that music could act as a gateway to things like alcohol, sex, and rebellion. I privately begged to differ. In fact, so driven by my love for music, I secretly went out and purchased a portable tape player, stashing it in my room. I was devout in my compliance with Islamic law, but my affection for music carved out a special place for this one single sin. I felt like a rebel approaching the counter, tapes in hand, buying a new album from some Lebanese pop artist.

Then at night, alone in bed, I would put on my headphones, pop in a tape, and hit play. The music was ecstasy. The melodies, rhythms, chords, and harmonies were transportive and contrasted so strongly with my daily life of scarce entertainment. Music was more than fun, it was *formative*. It was a window to a bigger world—it became my only escape! There under the covers, with a tape player in the dark, I became a rebellious symbol of resistance and personal autonomy.

In the Middle East, we learn to memorize things at a very young age—it's a cultural method of education. In studying music, for example, the Middle Eastern mind can carry notes longer than the Western mind due to being conditioned in memorization from very early on. I would lie in bed and listen, memorizing songs. When the album was

9. Haram means things that are unacceptable or illegal in Islamic law. The opposite would be Halal, which means in compliance with Islamic law.

over, I would flip the tape and play the other side, sinking back into a state of awe and wonder. When the headphones were off and the music was only a memory, a familiar guilt would creep in. I tried to justify myself internally to no avail. Occasionally, the shame was strong enough that I would stop and decide to get my life right, vowing to never listen to music again. I would go about my day resisting the temptation to hum those songs to myself when around others, which would reveal my secret sin.

The truth is, there was no room for fun. I was sheltered, controlled, and existed in a bubble where, in a big way, wrong was right and right was wrong. As a teen, I wanted to talk to guys, go out, and had an inborn curiosity about the world. These were not the base urges of a rebel bent on sin. It was the harmless, innocent curiosity of a teen exploring her world. I was underestimated and doubted by the elders, namely my uncles. The true depth of my potential and uniqueness was always present, but yet to be discovered.

I learned to live by outward deeds with little mention of the heart. Life under my mom's tutelage was very performance-driven. Achievements and accomplishments were the benchmarks of success, and emotional expression was often viewed as unnecessary or even a sign of weakness. Personal feelings and desires were usually sidelined.

My mother had a hard exterior shell about her. While my emotions were suppressed, hers often came out in a big way, especially anger, which was sometimes accompanied by a slap in the face. She had been battle-hardened by life and carried a general skepticism toward the world around her. She trusted very few people and taught us to doubt others as well. Cynicism and coldness were her mode of operation, yet in the midst of her unpredictable moods, I somehow became her golden child. More than my siblings, I looked like my mother, and she liked that very much. I felt I was being forged into an extension of her. She gave me education and opportunity and wanted me to go far in life, yet somehow her hopes and dreams for me felt like a personal achievement for her rather than a success for me. This self-involvement seemed to color all of my interactions with her.

Even now, I recall times when she would sit and cry, telling me about her issues and the troublesome happenings of her life. I would patiently listen and comfort her. The mother/daughter roles were reversed, and I found myself acting as a caretaker when a caretaker was what I needed as well. Nevertheless, I was her favorite and her go-to place to vent.

Being strong in school made me all the more favorable in her eyes. My academic success was a trophy she wore, as if her name was at the top of my papers as well. I began sensing envy from my siblings over my mother's special treatment of me, though they failed to see that it was not about me at all. As a reaction, I became an encourager to them and to others in general.

My peers began seeing me as a natural leader, though the term "female leader" was an oxymoron at the time. I had cousins and female friends who would secretly date without their parents knowing it, and I became a confidante and advisor to them, helping them dodge the watchful eyes of our elders. My ability to keep secrets and offer sensible advice made me a trusted ally. While I myself was not dating, I would listen to their stories, offer guidance on navigating relationships, and help them manage the delicate balance between modern dating and traditional expectations. It was thrilling, feeling like I was let into a secret mission.

Time passed, and I felt increasingly torn between my own dreams and the expectations of my culture. Here I was, a young Saudi teen, brimming with questions about the world, eager to explore its vastness and diversity. Yet, there was a clear barrier made up of the expectations of society.

My heart longed to unravel mysteries and to understand the stories and lives of others. I felt an innate pull to empower women and break free of norms. Each step toward self-discovery, however, felt like a step away from what I was supposed to be. Looking back, I realize how little I truly knew about myself. I lacked an awareness of my giftings and strengths. I did not know who I was or what I offered the world. My coverings seemed to shroud me, not only from God, but they separated me from myself. Why? Because my coverings were not merely a layer of physical black clothing but a layer of spiritual garb, keeping me from seeing and grasping the truth.

As I entered my high school years, I was caught in a whirlwind of competing interests, desires, options, and expectations. The traditional married life of a Saudi teen girl was soon to present itself as a viable option. The academic and career expectations of my mother would also be on the table. Beyond both of those things, a new door was soon to open, an opportunity that no one saw coming—including me.

CHAPTER FOUR

An Open Door

By the Hand of God

> *"In new surroundings, one grows new eyes."*
> —MARTY RUBIN

I heard a loud honk from the car outside. Panicked, I quickly scrambled to finish getting dressed. Another honk came, and then another. *How did I oversleep again?* When we first moved to Al-Qatif, my aunt arranged a pickup for us, a driver who would wait patiently outside. By now, though, we had shifted to a new school, and my uncles dropped us off daily.

With a racing heart, I finished donning my veil, and just as I was slipping on my shoes, the car was driving off in a cloud of dust down the road. I went outside, dejected, knowing I would be walking to school in the oppressive heat on sun-baked sidewalks. If we were not out the door in perfect time, our uncles ensured that a walk to school would become part of our morning routine. This happened several times. After making the unpleasant walk, passing the guard out front, and entering the all-female classroom, I could uncover and cool down.

In Saudi Arabia, we began with six elementary grades that started at age six. From there, we had three middle grades, which were punctuated by three years of secondary school—the equivalent of high school in the West. After that, one moves on to university. While in secondary school, I studied relentlessly. I was not just checking an academic box, but I knew that my marks would make a difference in my access to universities, career, and beyond. Being Shia certainly did not help in my schooling as Sunni teachers would poke at us, which at times became full-blown persecution—more on that later in the chapter.

I began seeing that history was not taught objectively in the classroom, but was revised and presented with certain nationalistic biases. We were told how great Saudi and the Arabs were, but learned very little of other nations. Anything we did learn about other countries was usually cast in a negative light while propping up the merits of our own nation and people. It was as though a rich world history had not existed outside the invisible boundaries of the Middle East. Later, I would have to re-educate myself on world history, reversing the indoctrination of my public schooling.

In the classroom, I noticed something else peculiar—a sort of misplaced affection. As teenage girls, our social lives almost exclusively existed among other girls. Young ladies had a natural desire for romance and a surplus of affection to give, with no one of the opposite sex to share it with. As a result, affection was expressed in ways that might seem unconventional by Western standards.

For instance, writing long love letters to a friend would have been a normal act. One might even bring a bouquet of flowers or express deep affection for a female teacher. Playing with hair or holding hands was quite normal between us, which on the surface might seem romantic. In actuality, nothing about the behavior was ever sexual in nature, but a manifestation of a need for emotional connection.

In a culture where overt displays of affection were limited in public, these gestures among friends became a language of love and acceptance. It was a way for young girls to navigate the complexities of our emotional landscapes, to find a sense of belonging. It was a natural response to a complete lack of actual dating culture. Romance with the opposite sex was not explored before marriage, and marriage itself was not some beautiful, movie-like *happily ever after.* Marriage in Islam was not a partnership but an arrangement where men control everything and women provide sex, childcare, and house care, like cooking and laundry. Men provided money and control while rarely having time with the children. I began to notice that even couples who had been married for decades seemed to know very little about one another. The cold and confined fate of a married woman scared me, and as I approached college age, I developed my biggest fear yet: the fear of being stuck in a bad marriage.

When I would discuss what my life would look like as I moved into college, my uncles were always quick to add, "Who cares about your schooling? You will end up staying home and following your husband anyway." They saw academics and career as a futile pursuit—a waste of time that only distracted from a woman's true calling within the home.

I protested on the inside, but remained silent on the outside. *You don't know me,* I thought. *This will never happen with me.* I wanted a partner, not a boss. Unfortunately, this was unthinkable in the eyes of Muslim men. Had I been born a few decades earlier, I may have had no choice but to enter a marriage with a tyrant of a husband. Arranged marriage was still the norm in my teen years, but now included the consent of the bride-to-be. This meant that I had the power to veto a proposal—and I often did.

In fact, in my teens and early twenties, I received about seven marriage proposals in total. They all came with different reasons and motives. One guy, for example, proposed to me because he was short and I'm fairly tall by Saudi standards. "This will give our children a chance to have decent height," he pleaded. Being a means to taller offspring is not exactly romantic. Everything about the utilitarian, domineering model of Muslim marriage made me anxious. I rejected every proposal without a second thought.

On the home front, I seemed to be stuck in a brutal cycle with my mother. She was a complicated figure, embodying both love and pain in equal measure. Our relationship seemed to exist between highs and lows. Over time, I became aware of a distinct pattern in how she related to me. For a season, I would be showered with affection and attention; some might call it *love bombing*. She would praise my achievements, making me feel like the most important person in her world. However, these periods of affection were short-lived and soon gave way to devaluation. It was as if a switch had been flipped, and the loving mother I knew transformed into a critical and dismissive figure. She would belittle my accomplishments, criticize my appearance, and undermine my confidence. Her words were sharp, cutting through my self-esteem like a knife. I felt as if I could never meet her expectations, and that I was always falling short of the ideal daughter she wanted.

This was generally followed by her detaching and becoming distant, which felt as though she had withdrawn her love and left me to navigate my teenage years alone. The absence of her affection was palpable, and I often felt abandoned and unworthy of care. Just when I thought the cycle was over, my mother would re-engage with me, initiating another round of highs and lows. It was a confusing and disorienting experience, as I was never sure which version of my mom I would encounter. The constant fluctuation between warmth and coldness left me feeling emotionally drained and unsure of my place in her world.

She wanted me to be formal, proper, professional, and to carry a sense of decorum. As I looked ahead to college and beyond, it was clear she wanted me to be a doctor. It was a good, highly paid job that came with status and prestige. As possibilities for women were slowly increasing, I could be a female pioneer in the field; my career could become her trophy.

As I closed out my final year of secondary school, the classes became more intense. The "senior year" of a Saudi student sets the trajectory of the rest of his or her life, so good grades are critical. Everyone takes it very seriously. Many women were finishing this final year and then promptly getting married, but my dreams differed. I always knew I would do something for women, but I felt I was in the wrong kingdom. I wanted to study and complete a PhD, earning the respect of men. I dreamt of launching a business or joining a large international firm and climbing the ranks in a corporation.

I longed to leave behind my country and explore the big, broad world. Whether it was simply crossing the bridge to Bahrain, or journeying to the United Arab Emirates or Jordan, I just wanted to get out. Areas of Europe, like London, felt like the farthest place I might venture to go to in a wild once-in-a-lifetime scenario, and anything west of that was an unrealistic pipe dream. Because I lacked the money, family support, and viable options, it seemed that I would be studying and starting my adult life in the same place I had grown up.

My mother persisted in her campaign to make me a doctor. She would state the endless reasons why this was the best path and give not-so-subtle guilt trips if any other path was chosen on my part. The problem is, I was afraid of blood, which happens to be a pretty big issue when pursuing a future in medicine. However, I acquiesced. And shortly after graduating from secondary school, I began applying for colleges to become a doctor.

* * *

Saudi Arabia is rife with college options for men. Every major city is full of male universities, training up the next generation of leaders who will expand the vision and influence of the oil-based state. For women, however, the options are limited, which makes the college selection process frustrating. In part, I wanted to be a man, get a degree, then go back to being a woman after four years when I had gotten my education. It would certainly make things easier.

Both my gender and my Shia background were working against me as a sort of cruel double persecution. Despite being at the top of my class and getting a 97 out of 100 on my final grades in secondary school, I was rejected from several universities. After three or four rejection letters came in, I was shocked and saddened. I knew non-Shia girls with lower GPAs who were accepted, while I was left out.

One school replied, "We have rejected your application because we want you to study chemistry, then pharmacy, and after that, we can accept you to study to be a doctor." In truth, this entire pursuit was my mother's idea to begin with. Frustrated and worn out, I decided to dig my heels into the process and study chemistry. I hated it with a passion but stayed the course for the entire semester, knowing pharmacology and med school awaited me on the other side. I studied with great fervor and dedication—memorizing atoms, compounds, elements, and how they relate to one another. As the semester came to a close, I would be traveling to Riyadh, the capital city of Saudi Arabia, to take my final exams.

The city was a sprawling metropolis. The journey was a mix of anticipation and worry, a blend of excitement for the new experiences that lay ahead and the looming pressure of the final exam that had brought me there. The sheer size of the city struck me. Skyscrapers towered over the city, glinting in the twilight. The roads were wider, the traffic denser, and the pace of life seemed faster, as if the city itself was pulsating with energy and ambition.

The buildings had sleek designs and innovative architecture, which stood as a testament to Saudi Arabia's rapid development. Like many Middle Eastern capitals, the city embraced the future while still holding onto its cultural heritage. It was an imposing and beautiful skyline.

My mind, however, was preoccupied with the exam that awaited me. It was more than just a test; it was a culmination of years of hard work and a gateway to future opportunities. I felt a deep sense of responsibility, not only to myself but to my mother. Riyadh, with all its complexity and beauty, was now the backdrop for one of the more significant tests of my schooling thus far.

The test was administered, and the results were given that same day. When the scores were finally revealed, mine was impressively high. The diligence had paid off, and I did quite well. Yet, despite this achievement, I was met with a disheartening reality: I was not accepted. The disappointment was overwhelming, and I left the examiners' room in tears, my hopes seemingly shattered.

Outside, a scene unfolded that would leave an indelible mark on my heart. A woman stood there with her daughter, who, despite a significantly lower score than mine, had been accepted. As I emerged, my tears visible, the woman met my gaze with a look of profound empathy. She saw how I was treated as a Shia was discriminatory and wrong. Her words, which she then spoke, resonated deep within my soul: "If God closes one door, He will open another. Everything works for good to those who love Him. I know it's not just and it's not fair. Go have lunch and enjoy yourself, knowing God has something better."

Her words were a balm to my wounded heart. She extended her hand, offering me 50 riyal. In that moment, her encouragement and faith infused me with a newfound sense of hope and strength. Despite the injustice and the tears, her words reminded me that life's path is often unpredictable, but always purposeful for those who keep faith.

"Who are you?" I asked.

She explained that she had lived in the US and had studied special needs education. She came back to reverse the stigma in the Middle East that special needs children, according to Islam, are cursed. This thinking has led them to be forgotten with a lack of care and attention. Her time abroad introduced her to a more compassionate and wholesome way of viewing the world. She was either a Christian or at least exposed to Christian values. At times, I wonder if she might have been an angel.

I departed, but her words did not depart from me. I had a good friend there that day who was also rejected due to being a Shia, and we left to have lunch at a big mall in the area. It was as though a switch had been flipped, and I suddenly left my medical dreams behind without a hint of nostalgia for them. With an encouraging word from a stranger in my soul, my tears were dry, and I quickly moved on to the next dream as we ate and talked.

Upon returning home, my mother was upset with the results, though she took the opportunity to bring shame and express skepticism, asking, "Are you *sure* you got a good score?" In her world, if I had gotten a 99%, I was to blame because I did not get a 100%.

In the wake of my initial setback, I found myself at a crossroads, thinking deeply about my future. *What do I truly enjoy? What direction do I want my life to take?* These questions echoed in my mind as I sought to carve a new path for myself.

Being the first in my family to own a laptop, I always had a fascination with computers. This interest sparked the idea that perhaps my future would be in the field of computer science. With this newfound prospect, I set my sights on a modest school—a bridge school of sorts, newly established and lacking the prestige of more renowned universities. Yet, it was a place where I felt I could begin laying the groundwork for my degree.

My academic journey there was relatively smooth; the classes weren't particularly challenging. However, the experience was unique in its own right. We, the students, often felt like subjects in an educational experiment. Because it was a new school, our classroom settings shifted and changed as the leadership continued to evolve and find their footing.

After completing a year in this transitional phase, I made a significant move—relocating to the capital city, Riyadh, to continue studying IT. Here, my classes were not just specialized in computers but included female Gen Ed courses like cooking, Arabic, sewing, and so forth. I would often escape the monotony of classes by exploring online chat rooms. They transported me beyond the borders of the nation I seemed to be stuck in. During that time, MSN Messenger was a major player in this space and offered chat rooms by topic and interests.

I could pass hours and hours talking with men and women from near and far about all of the various subjects under the sun. It was a place where my curiosity could be satisfied and my internal borders expanded. I had the cover of anonymity, as most of us used fake usernames.

At one point, I had begun a conversation with a guy from my city. The talks were always polite and insightful, but I did not foresee that they might become life-altering in any way. I had mentioned to him prior that I dreamt of one day leaving the country and exploring something new. Of course, I knew this was only a dream—a far-fetched one at that.

Some time later, out of the blue, he messaged me a link to a website. Curious, I clicked the URL and was taken to a landing page that announced a new education program that had been developed by the Saudi government. My heart raced as I read on. The program would allow Saudi students to travel abroad to complete their college education. Not only that, but the scholarship would *completely* cover tuition, room and board, the cost of living, student visas, and all travel expenses related to the move. I saw a new future being born before my eyes.

I thanked him for the tip, closed the chat, and immediately made plans to apply.

* * *

It was the summer of 2005, and at that time, the demographics of Saudi Arabia were lopsided. Around 70% of the population was under the age of 30. Throughout Europe and the rest of the world, this number was closer to 50%. Why did this create a problem for the Saudi government? Because this youthful majority would soon be taking the reins and leading the dominant Saudi oil industry. The problem was that the Saudi education system had some serious shortcomings. As a result, industry leaders were continually hiring foreign experts who had been educated in Europe and America. In short, Saudi Arabia's own citizens were not prepared for these critical native roles.

Amidst this backdrop, the leader at the time, known affectionately as Baba Abdulla | بابا عبد الله, or "Father Abdullah," created this scholarship. King Abdullah was a unifier who transcended the sectarian divide, treating Shia and Sunni alike with fairness for all. He understood the value of studying abroad. In fact, royal families in the Middle East are often educated in Europe, learning in a world far removed from the life of the average Saudi citizen.

Taking my first course in International Relations, I learned that the King Abdullah Scholarship Program was actually initiated with the encouragement of a U.S. diplomat (a Foreign Service Officer) after 9/11. At the time, relations between Saudi Arabia and the United States were strained because most of the men who carried out the attacks were Saudi citizens. In an effort to rebuild trust and strengthen ties, the U.S. suggested an educational exchange program. The idea was to give young Saudis the opportunity to study in the West, interact with Americans, and experience life in a democratic society with people of different beliefs.

This discovery was profound for me, since I had never known this—even after living in the U.S. for years. In April 2005, Crown Prince (later King) Abdullah bin Abdulaziz met with President George W. Bush at the Bush family ranch in Crawford, Texas. The two leaders issued a joint statement reaffirming their commitment to the U.S.–Saudi relationship, focusing on fighting terrorism, promoting stability in the Middle East, and expanding educational and cultural exchanges. One of the key outcomes was the launch of the King Abdullah Scholarship Program, which allowed Saudi students to study abroad and extended student visas to five years. It also enabled their families to visit on tourist visas, making the program more accessible and sustainable.

Abdula was interested in having this burgeoning group of Saudi youth bring skills and competency back to the nation after graduating. This would position the oil enterprise to continue to be dominant on a global scale. He so believed in this idea that he backed it with massive government funds. In fact, as of today, billions upon billions have been poured into Saudi education.

As I browsed the application, I saw they offered *so* many options to choose from. I could go almost anywhere I wanted. Despite hearing negative things about the United States as a nation, it had been ingrained in me that they *did* have the best college education system in the world. After all, I was not going in order to be taught morals and ethics by the U.S.—I was going for a college degree. Beyond that, my older sister had a brother-in-law who was studying in the U.S. While I did not know him personally, I reasoned he had made a good choice. I learned that he was attending a school in Louisiana, and figured I would follow suit.

I ignored every other nation listed and officially applied for a scholarship with the Saudi Government to attend school in the USA. From there, I completed my separate application for Louisiana State University, majoring in computer science. I waited patiently to hear back. In discussing the possibility with my mother, I found her to be surprised and happy about my chance to study abroad. She had raised us herself, overcome obstacles in life, and likely felt that having a daughter receive a good foreign education would somehow bring her honor.

Given my isolated upbringing, I knew nothing about Louisiana. Somewhere in my mind, I assumed that Louisiana, California, and New York were all close together and roughly the same in terms of culture, climate, and feel. Oh, how misguided I was. The sheer size of the United States and the countless differences from state to state had not yet come to my attention.

It was a unique year for the scholarship. Because it was just getting started, everyone who applied and met the requirements was accepted. Next, I just needed to receive an acceptance letter from the university. For international students, it is called an I-20, which is a multi-purpose document issued by a government-approved U.S. educational institution certifying that you have been admitted to a full-time program of study. I received mine in short order, the top of the page marked with the thrilling words: "Congratulations! You have been admitted to Louisiana State University for the 2006 Spring semester."

After that, my task was to simply take the I-20 to the Saudi embassy, and they would arrange to pay the school directly and begin setting up my F-1 student visa and travel arrangements. During the process, I had to visit the U.S. Consulate for a photograph for the F-1. This posed an issue. Shia women wear their hijabs differently than Sunnis, with more of their face being covered around the chin and with no hair showing whatsoever. The problem is, the photograph called for some of my hair and the top part of my forehead to be shown. The American worker was quite rude, informing me that he did not approve of my picture because no hair was showing.

In a harsh tone, I told him, "I am a Muslim. I cannot show my hair."

He proceeded to close the curtain on my face. A Moroccan man got out of his desk and spoke to me in Arabic, "Don't worry about showing your hair...we only need a little bit of it in the picture. These are the requirements."

Not wanting to lose my opportunity, I had to violate my own standards and retake the photos, some hair in frame, to finish processing the F-1 visa.

With the embassy taking care of the rest of the formalities, I was left to marvel at the reality of my dreams coming true. The idea of moving to the USA came with a whirlwind of emotions. It was surreal, almost like stepping into a vibrant painting that was once just a figment of my imagination. My heart raced with excitement at the thought of walking through the sprawling campus. I imagined myself, a girl from the Middle East, now embarking on a journey across oceans to a land of new accents, flavors, and traditions.

The excitement was palpable. I was about to dive into a sea of opportunities, to learn not just academically, but culturally, and to grow not just in knowledge, but in experience. The prospect of meeting people from all over the world, sharing stories, and making memories in a place so different from home was exhilarating. It felt like the beginning of a grand adventure, one where I would be the protagonist of my own story, exploring, learning, and evolving along the way.

As I lay in bed at night, my mind buzzed with thoughts of attending lectures, participating in events, and seeing new places. This was more than just an education; it was the opening chapter of a new life. Not only was my tuition paid, but I had an allowance that fully covered living expenses like rent, food, transport, and personal month-to-month costs. Untethered from money constraints, I was free to live and learn.

Amidst the excitement and anticipation, a thread of anxiety also wove its way through my thoughts. The prospect of leaving behind everything familiar was daunting. I wrestled with the realization that I would be thousands of miles away from the streets I knew. The big malls, familiar culture, and arid heat would all soon be replaced by the unknown.

Would I adapt to the American way of life? How would I navigate the stark contrasts between the conservative culture I grew up in and the more liberal environment I was heading towards? The thought of overcoming language barriers, understanding social norms, and establishing my identity in a diverse community was overwhelming. In quieter moments, I worried about the small things, too. Would I be able to find Halal food that suited our strict Islamic diet? How would I navigate the public transportation system? Or did one even exist?

Safety concerns also surfaced. My uncles on my dad's

side (who did not have legal authority over me) still tried to discourage me by painting awful pictures of American universities. "You know rape occurs at such a high rate in America?" they would say. "It happens in schools all the time, and you'll be all alone." This warning, paired with our media's portrayal of life in America, caused genuine fear for me. My four uncles would sit and argue over decisions, big and small, and my move to the U.S. certainly sparked debate. The reason being, in order for me to leave the country, I had to have male approval as a legal requirement. Gaining the approval of my eldest uncle would be the last barrier[10].

The week I got my paperwork to leave Saudi, a man attempted a last-minute proposal through one of my uncles. The guy had a master's degree from a school in Canada and promised to buy me a big house, to get me a driver, and to provide endless funds for me to shop with when I wasn't at home with the kids.

"Can I travel?" I asked.

"No, not without my permission," he said.

"And will *you* travel?"

"Yes, with my guy friends."

"No," was my instant answer. My mind was made up; I just needed the proper permission to get out of the country. I approached my eldest uncle to see about his approval. He was a respected figure in our family whose word was final.

---

10. Some Saudi women will forge this permission slip or pay someone in government due to their family not allowing them to leave.

Because my younger uncles were discouraging the move, I was uncertain how my eldest uncle would respond. With a steady gaze, he declared to me, "You will go. Nobody can oppose this decision. You're smart, Sahar." My other uncles could say nothing to refute the decision.

I was overwhelmed and surprised by the sense of validation and support.

He then completed the paper, granting me freedom to travel. The slip read, "Sahar is authorized to travel anywhere, at any time." Surprised, I asked him why he chose such broad terms.

"Perhaps you might want to explore other countries while you are studying in the U.S.," he explained, a hint of foresight in his voice. This permission allowed me to leave the Saudi airport to travel to any nation freely. This was uncharacteristically generous and forward-thinking of him. Looking back, I see that God was working in him to serve His purposes, influencing my uncle to play this crucial role in the unfolding of my destiny. His approval was not just a permission; it was a blessing that opened the doors to a world of possibilities.

Despite some angst that would come and go, my default state was one of absolute excitement. I knew I had a once-in-a-lifetime opportunity in front of me, and I was not going to miss it. The West awaited me. The question remained: Would I just be changing locations or changing in ways deeper than I could have imagined? I would soon find out.

CHAPTER FIVE

The New World

Hello Adventure!

"America is another name for opportunity."
—Ralph Waldo Emerson

I touched down in the USA on January 1st, 2006, five months after receiving my I-20. I had passed the time in shopping malls and clothing stores, buying an array of vibrant hijabs, dresses, and pants to wear underneath. I bought coats and packed sweaters, gearing up for the frigid cold.

Packing was a process of balancing the practical and the sentimental. It was a tug-of-war, deciding what to bring along and what to leave behind. I wound up with three suitcases, jammed completely full, mostly clothes, along with some books I loved, with the Quran, of course. One of my strengths has always been futuristic thinking and planning, so I was very much in my sweet spot as I sketched the days ahead in my daydreams. Most of my fears were hushed by my excitement, though I had never traveled alone, which made me a little nervous. Growing up, we had flown to Syria and traveled to Bahrain, but I was always with family. This time, I would be solo.

The day I left, I recall my sister's face and the tears streaming from her eyes. The family was tender, and I felt a swarm of positive and negative emotions. It was a heavy departure, as I did not know when I would see them again. My uncle on my dad's side picked me up for the trip to the airport. He strained lifting my enormous suitcase, "What do you have in here, Sahar?!"

"My iron," I said.

"You don't think they have irons in America?"

I shrugged. He took it out; having studied in the U.S. back in the day, he knew the power outlets there wouldn't accept my electronics anyway.

With my bags loaded, we made the drive to King Fahd International Airport. As we neared the departures, I was caught off guard by my uncle's last-minute attempt to derail my journey. "Please don't go alone, Sahar. Wait for your younger brother."

The mixture of pressure and angst swelled in my soul, knowing my response would not please him. He continued, "Your brother will finish school in two years—go with him then."

I politely explained that the time was not then but *now*. The opportunity may not exist for me in two years, and my move was irreversible. He seemed to understand the inevitability of my situation. We found the counter for KLM Royal Dutch Airlines and checked my bags. I was scheduled to hop from Riyadh to Holland, where their small European airport would be a stark contrast to the big, sweeping structures in Saudi Arabia. From Holland, I would fly to Washington, D.C.

As the first leg of the trip began, the plane took off, and the tan earth below became covered by the white clouds we entered. The familiar landscape of Saudi Arabia shrank into the distance, and a sense of finality overwhelmed me. Up until that point, I had not cried—not even during the goodbyes to my family—but the reality of leaving my home, my culture, and everything I knew hit me with unexpected force as I sat in my window seat. My eyes, which had been dry, now brimmed with tears. With each mile the plane covered, I felt a chapter of my life closing and a new one beginning, filled with both hope and apprehension.

* * *

My stomach now growled as I sat in my hotel room. The hunger one feels after extended travel is a unique sort of hunger, and I was deep in the throes of it. It appeared I would be fasting my first meal in America, but not for religious reasons.

I had arrived in DC earlier in the day, and a Saudi man had picked me up from the airport to take me to the consulate. There, I checked in and confirmed my arrival. The man had offered to get me food, but I was so shy I rejected the invitation. I had never driven in a car alone with a stranger, let alone a strange man. He was kind, but I remained suspicious, and as a result, I now sat in my room absolutely famished. I had no idea how to order food, let alone how to ensure it was halal | حلال.[11] I knew Americans ate pork, which was strictly forbidden, and I did not want to risk the cross-contamination of something unclean. So I slept hungry, and in the morning, the same man picked me up to finish more paperwork at the consulate.

The staff kindly showed me, with step-by-step instructions, how to open an American bank account and how to initiate a transfer of money from the Saudi government for personal expenses. They applied for my health insurance and gave practical insight as I settled into life in the West.

They were truly rolling out the red carpet, spoiling me with the finest treatment imaginable.

After wrapping up the logistics, I was taken back to Dulles, where I would finish the last leg of the journey to Baton Rouge. Classes would begin in less than two weeks. A driver was arranged to take me from the airport to the apartment complex near the University where I would be living. Upon

---

11. Halal food is "permitted" food that is prepared with strict guidelines. The Islamic method of slaughtering animals or poultry, dhabiha, involves killing through a cut to the jugular vein, carotid artery, and windpipe. Animals must be alive and healthy at the time of slaughter and all blood is drained from the carcass.

arriving in Louisiana, a cold blast of air smacked me in the face. I instantly noticed the bitter cold. Even with my thick winter coat, a scarf, a hat, and wool gloves, I found myself shivering from the frigid air.

It was 60 degrees Fahrenheit.

I was accustomed to having a driver take me anywhere I wanted to go, so commuting on foot between my apartment and the nearby campus was an adjustment. Walking through the 2,000-acre campus for the first time, I was awestruck by its sheer size—it was like a city in itself. The sprawling grounds were dotted with impressive buildings, each with unique architecture, ranging from classic brick to more modern structures. The air was filled with the sounds of chattering students and the distant laughter from nearby groups.

The ancient oak trees were majestic, towering high above with their empty January branches spreading wide. With spring on the way, there would soon be a canopy of shade, and the grass would become green and full, covering the campus like a plush carpet. Nearly everything contrasted with the desert I had always known. The University Lakes were encircled with walking trails and paths for bikers and joggers. There was no shortage of places to study and pass the time.

Most of what I knew about America I had learned from shows like *Full House* or from watching permitted Hollywood movies. I was not sure how my experience would match with these programs. I quickly realized that Baton Rouge is not New York City and that cultures and accents vary greatly from one place to the next in America. I noticed the way people spoke in Louisiana was different from what I had seen on television, with the southern drawl and colloquialisms.

For my first year in college, I was scheduled to take English classes exclusively, which was beneficial for two reasons. First, I needed formal education to improve my accent, reading, and writing. And second, it meant I was able to meet lots of international students who were doing the same thing.

I found myself amidst a melting pot of cultures and perspectives, a far cry from the homogeneity I was accustomed to in Saudi Arabia. The only other time I had seen such diversity was in my distant childhood while living in Khafji. At LSU, I met people from every corner of the globe—Argentina, Kurdistan, China, and beyond. One of the most memorable was a girl from Turkey, also a Muslim, who chose not to cover herself. This sparked debates between us about the true essence of our faith and the practice of covering. To my chagrin, I did not win her over.

I also developed a friendship with a guy from Italy, who often lamented the quality of pasta in the USA. He regularly received shipments of olive oil straight from Italy, and his passion for authentic Italian cuisine was infectious. I remember being invited to his home, where he cooked incredible pasta dishes. He spoke with passion, pinching his fingers together with that distinctive Italian gesture. It was a wonderful glimpse into his culture and the pride he took in the beloved food from his homeland.

Another friend from Argentina was endlessly curious about Islam, particularly the practice of covering. He playfully suggested that maybe I didn't have hair at all, and once asked a female classmate to accompany me to the bathroom to verify my hair's existence. He asked, "Will I ever see your hair before I return to Argentina?" To which I replied with a smile, "No, you won't."

I may have been in America, but I was not going to be *Americanized*.

The culture among the students was quite the shock, with frequent parties and bustling nightlife—especially considering I came from a nation where alcohol itself was banned. On one occasion, a man stopped me on campus for a survey: "Would you have sex before marriage?" It was the wrong question to ask a devout Muslim woman.

"No," I responded.

"But how can you tell what flavor you like if you don't try before marriage?" he prodded.

Instances like these served as a stark reminder that I was no longer in the chaste Middle East. I remained devout and knew my stay in the USA was short-term, which gave me comfort. I viewed the nation as mostly dishonoring to God and did not think I could be happy in a place like this long term given the loose standards. The more I learned about American social life, the more I viewed it as morally bankrupt.

I began group study with American girls to help me with English on a weekly basis, where I would cook for them before reading and going over classwork. In Saudi Arabia, you simply did not have people over to your house without preparing food of some sort—it was to be expected. I was surprised to learn this was not the standard in the West. I recall spending hours preparing a big dish only to hear, "No thanks, I ate at home," when my guests arrived.

Likewise, when I would visit them at their apartments, I was caught off guard to not be offered so much as water or tea. Apparently, "southern hospitality" had not made its way onto the campuses of Louisiana State. Nevertheless, I adjusted and kept my opinions to myself. With these few friends, I did feel I was being kept at arm's length from them in some ways. This was confirmed when one night, two of them came knocking at my door. They staggered in when I opened the door, and it was evident that both of them were drunk. Wreaking of alcohol, they laughed, joked, and kissed one another.

"What is going on here?" I asked, trying to hide my utter astonishment.

"Oh...we didn't tell you, we're lesbians."

I had never heard of such a phrase and proceeded to Google it from my phone.

"Don't judge us," one of them said.

"I won't judge you, just don't touch me."

They eventually left, and I remained ever suspicious of the Western way of living. The last thing I wanted was to be influenced by the debauchery that I saw on campus. I maintained a sense of apprehension toward the American norms around me. In fact, even after several months, I was haunted by my uncle's comment about sexual assault in the States and was afraid of entering public bathrooms alone.

Eventually, by time and experience, I gathered that the nation was far safer than previously described to me, though I still disliked the promiscuous lifestyles I was seeing around me. Being someone who steered clear of parties in a place where they were happening every Friday and Saturday, my weekends often felt isolating. It was a lonesome season, fraught with challenges, and there were moments when I felt utterly alone. Nevertheless, I understood that I had no choice but to persevere. I had a goal in mind and would not stop until it was achieved.

* * *

"For this assignment," our professor began, "I'd like you to write a comparative essay of your home country's culture and American culture. Examine how those cultural norms, values, traditions, and behaviors contrast and align."

Easy. I had endless material, though I majored on one particular difference: In the USA, it seemed that when a child reached 18 years of age, they were nearly pushed out of the house. If a young person lived at home beyond this and into their twenties, it almost seemed taboo at the time. In Saudi, families stayed together longer with a more communal living arrangement. We did not equate living at home with freeloading or laziness by default. It seemed that many of my American friends felt disowned, like they were free to visit for the holidays, but otherwise, they had to forge their path in life by themselves.

The downside of the close-knit, communal living that I had been accustomed to was the sense of control. The head of the home could very well be a tyrant, and a child often lived under those conditions for many years longer than they would in the States. Nevertheless, I truly missed the communal sense of sharing and closeness that I knew.

In response, my teacher praised the essay and noted, "Sahar, this is true for many homes in the U.S., but not true in mine. My children always have a room in my house. Always." I found her affirmation to be comforting. In fact, I always noticed when Americans did or said something that reminded me of home. A comment, a meal, a sight, a joke, or a situation could act as a portal, transporting me back to the rhythms of Qatif, giving me a moment of sweet nostalgia while abroad.

In my studies, I found myself enjoying the English language very much. I loved reading English books and examining the sentences, which were so different from Arabic.

Like Hebrew, Arabic is a Semitic language that reads from right to left. Our alphabet is entirely different from English, which means we not only have to learn pronunciations and vocabulary, but we must start by learning a new twenty-six letter alphabet from scratch.

In Arabic, we often tell our thoughts in the form of a story. Jesus, for example, gave parabolic teaching, and we do the same today throughout the Middle East. After moving to the States, I would attempt to think in Arabic and write in English, but quickly found that it did not work. The two languages simply were not cohesive, so it felt like I was in a sort of verbal childhood all over again. Grammar was hard, and pronunciation was a strain. It took me quite some time to become completely fluent, and my accent was much thicker in those early days.

I stuck with it. An article I read on language mentioned that if you develop your listening, you can better develop your speaking. During my downtime, I watched loads of movies with subtitles, pausing to write down words I did not know, repeating them out loud before continuing the film.

I made a point to master local idioms and phrases. People in America say, "I see," while you're explaining something, which completely threw me for a loop at first. *You see? What do you see? Can I see it too?* I would think to myself. Phrases like *play it by ear* or *break a leg* all had to be deciphered and memorized. It took much time, but being immersed in the culture was an incredible help that expedited my learning process in a way that could not have happened by merely taking English courses back home.

I had one male teacher who was quite strict about our pronunciation. As a Saudi woman, I was already very shy around male teachers. It took years to adjust to this new dynamic of mixed genders in an academic setting. Nevertheless, he was quite forward in his approach. On one occasion, he was determined to correct my pronunciation of the letter "p". In Arabic, we simply do not have a "p" sound of any kind. As a result, people from our part of the world say things like *beoble* instead of *people*. To correct this, my teacher held a piece of paper in front of my face.

"Air should come out of your mouth when you make the 'p' sound. You need to make the sound hard enough to move my paper with air. If the paper does not move, you're still stuck on the 'b' sound."

Sure enough, it worked. As uncomfortable as I might have been, the paper moved, and my accent improved. Pronunciations did not come easily, and neither did the use of language. On one occasion, a friend was going through a breakup, and I decided to comfort her with kind words that would surely act as a balm for the soul.

"You are a strange, strange woman. You can handle this," I said.

Wiping tears, she said, "What? Why are you calling me strange?!"

Turns out, *strange* and *strong* sound more similar than Western ears might realize, and calling someone a strange independent woman is not exactly a compliment. While some stories from my adjustment in the USA are funny and light, such as this one, others are more alienating. During the hot Louisiana summer, men seeing my hijab would call out, "It's hot out, take off your scarf!" I had no response, and comments like this felt like a jab, rather than actual curiosity or concern.

In class, I made an interesting discovery: The main factor in my feeling alienated was not the comments of insensitive Westerners. It was not the Islamic fundamentalists who took issue with the coloration of my hijab. Instead, it was the cold and subtle experience of being ignored at a polite distance. During group projects, pods of students would form around the lecture hall, and I found myself alone with no one asking me to join. Professors, noticing this, would then move to integrate me with existing groups. As we worked out roles and assignments, I was spoken to very little by the other students, which hurt me deeply.

In truth, my classmates were not going out of their way to be rude or hurtful. I believe they simply did not know what to do with me. They likely wondered about language barriers, cultural norms, and might have even feared stepping out of line. Many Westerners feel hesitant when they see a hijab or religious garb. There are so many preconceived notions and mental templates that we use while engaging with others. The solution, at the end of the day, is honest, humble communication.

If you are a Western person wondering how to engage with Muslims, know that you do not have to walk on eggshells. They are not sitting on the edge of their seats just waiting to be offended by American inquiry. Ask questions and broach topics. Bring up conversation and treat people as individuals. Muslims are more open than you'd think, and they quite like talking about God, theology, culture, and worldviews. Listen to their stories about their upbringing, their values. Everyone has their own unique perspective and sets of ideas, including Muslims, so lean in and hear theirs.

At the end of the day, people do not want to feel like a project or like you are required to tiptoe around them. Things like politics and religion might be hush-hush topics in the West, but are subjects we love talking through and debating in the East. Should you ask about traditions, head coverings, or rituals, Muslims won't be offended; most will be honored. So much of the distance created between cultures, religions, races, and nationalities is not born out of hate but hesitation. It's easier to avoid what we don't understand rather than engage in it. The tragedy in this is that engaging diverse cultures and backgrounds can lead to rich understanding and can open doors to vibrant communication.

I must say, there are a few people in the U.S. who fully

understood this. One of my professors made it very clear that she cared for us as students beyond the classroom. She took us to the movies, brought us into her home for meals, and asked us interesting questions. She not only made me feel welcomed but also gave me a sense of belonging that made a lasting difference. Without her, my time at LSU would have been far less meaningful.

Several months had passed on campus, and I grew curious about the rest of the United States. Knowing there were transfer options available, I became open to the idea of new destinations, new people, and new paths.

CHAPTER SIX

Challenger

Questioning the Status Quo

"Be a free thinker and don't accept everything you hear as truth."
—SOCRATES

The check was for $3,000, and I was both elated and confused in equal measure. Why on earth would LSU write *me* a check? I approached the administrative offices of the University and inquired. It turns out, the money transfer system between the Saudi government and universities was not very precise. As foreigners, we were already paying three times more than the locals, yet the Saudi government kept sending overpayments on behalf of students. The school quickly realized that sending a refund to a student on campus is easier than trying to figure out how to mail a check to the government of Saudi Arabia. Opting for simplicity over bureaucratic entanglements, they simply gave the overpayments to students.

Each time a new check showed up, I would let the university know, and they would inform me to, "Just keep it." *If you insist*, I thought. Even after graduation, these unintended gifts rolled in and, in total, I received somewhere around $5,000 in overpayment funds during my time in school. It seemed that beyond tuition, housing, and personal expenses, unexpected provision was showing up and facilitating a comfortable life in a setting that was sometimes *uncomfortable*.

My first year was overshadowed by bouts of severe homesickness. I longed for familiar comforts and relief from the feeling of being the odd woman out. I would cry and call my mother for consolation. I had the option for a paid trip home in the summer, but chose not to as I wanted to finish my English courses over break. My schedule was to study English for the first year and then dive into my computer science major after that, and a trip home meant my graduation would be delayed. I was already an older student who had bounced around majors in Saudi and felt behind. The price of graduating in a timely manner was studying rather than visiting home. I pined for the small joys of the Middle East—the bread, pastries, and sweets from the local bakeries. Quickly, I found that bread in the U.S. was heavily processed, and I became bloated and gained weight. I adopted a mostly vegetarian diet and did my best to adjust to the newness of it all.

At the time, I had two cousins studying at Chico State in California. They were not blood cousins, but our moms were close friends. While I knew their names, I didn't know them personally. Given that we were all in the U.S., my mom made a suggestion, "Why don't you Skype them?"—tinged with the usual Saudi pronunciation that sounded more like *Skyb-ee.*

We set up the introductory call.

"What are you doing in Louisiana?" they asked.

"I don't know…I thought all of America was pretty close together," I said, revealing my naiveté.

"Sahar, you already have a Saudi accent. Soon, you will have a Saudi *and* southern accent. Come to Chico with us."

They gave their reasons and described the area. I thought through the logistics of the move and inquired about the transfer of credits. Eventually, they convinced me and even helped me obtain a transfer paper to send to the Saudi embassy, ensuring tuition payments would be seamlessly rerouted.

With just an eight-month history in Louisiana behind me, I boxed and shipped all of my furniture and possessions over 2,000 miles to Northern California. My cousins picked me up from the airport in Sacramento, marking the start of a rich adult friendship. While our mothers had been close, I had no time with them in childhood, so it was our first meeting. I was on the shy side, a little nervous, but warmed up quickly. They cooked for me on the first night, showed the usual Saudi hospitality, and even let me stay in a spare bedroom while I got settled with new housing.

I was eager to immerse myself in a culture that differed from the South. Chico, with its quaint charm and diversity, promised just that and more. I could sense that the area had a deeper understanding and appreciation for the world and its various cultures. The town's small scale fostered a sense of community and belonging that was cozy and welcoming. It wasn't just a place to study; it was a place to grow, to interact, and to belong. It was in this setting that my worldview would be challenged and put to the test.

The school itself, nestled in this idyllic setting, had a vibrant campus life. I was beginning to feel less like a student from a far-off land and more like a part of the fabric of the culture. The transition was smoother than anticipated. I loved the mild weather and California sun. I felt I could occupy this wonderful corner of the world for the duration of my education, and I did.

Early on, I met a man named Hussein, also from the Middle East, who became like a brother to me. He was compassionate, kind, and grew up with many sisters, and treated me like one of his own. On many occasions, he helped me with homework, would bring me food, or give me advice on cultural subjects. It was pure, platonic care, and I truly valued our connection.

With my English courses behind me, I was now ready for programming and computer science classes, which were extremely hard. Frankly, it was by the help of Hussein and my cousins (who also majored in MIS) that I wound up graduating. The coding was remarkably difficult. If the smallest comma was out of place, the entire code was dead on arrival. After a semester of computer science, I decided to make a change. If I had my pick of majors, I would have studied fashion or international business. Unfortunately, the Saudi government limited the major choices for the scholarship. Most of the options involved management, IT, and so forth. Naturally, they wanted to get a return on their investment, so they empowered their people to study what was lacking in the homeland. They needed tech innovators and managers, not clothing designers—France and Italy had that covered.

I switched to and stuck with a Management and Information Systems major, which felt fitting and more in my line of interest. I loved the management classes, and business law 101 was quite interesting. In fact, I considered switching to study law, which was also on the table, but changing again would put me even further behind. The math courses were a breeze, and I even took French as a foreign language, which I thoroughly enjoyed.

During Ramadan that year, I recall walking with my brother on campus. By then, he was also a student at CSU. For this 30-day period, we fasted from dawn to sunset with no food or water, facing Al-Kaaba | الكعبة [12] while praying throughout the day. As we walked the campus, we were confronted by men with signs, yelling that we were going to hell for not accepting Jesus. I hated the feeling it gave me, seeing anger and condemnation in their eyes toward us. We felt targeted. Maybe he was fueled by religious zeal or perhaps he was just irritable from being tired and hungry, but my brother approached and responded frankly with, "We are fasting to please our God. *You* are the ones who are going to hell!"

The vitriol was not unique to so-called Christians. I recall Saudi men in the States who rebuked me for wearing a colorful head scarf and angrily encouraged the all-black garb seen throughout Saudi. It was a sort of double judgment where Westerners viewed me as ultra-religious and my own people saw me as ultra-liberal and progressive. Caught between persecution on both sides, I seemed to be incapable of pleasing either party.

I did find a welcoming touchpoint, however, at the local mosque, though it came from an unexpected source. Shortly after moving, one of my priorities was to find a place of worship, and Chico had a couple of options for Muslims. There, in the heart of a foreign land, where the tapestry of life seemed unfamiliar and daunting, I had the fortune of

---

12. Sometimes called Al-Kaaba Al-Musharrafa | الكعبة المشرفة, it is a stone building at the center of Islam's most important mosque and holiest site, the Masjid al-Haram in Mecca, Saudi Arabia.

crossing paths with Janet, an American woman of Catholic faith, whose heart seemed to go beyond the boundaries of religion and culture.

Her husband was a teacher at CSU, and after seeing so many Muslims attending, his wife felt inspired to make us feel welcome. Despite the ocean of differences that lay between us—age, faith, and background—we found a common ground as human beings. Janet was naturally curious and not threatened by Islam. Instead, she was invested in it, maintaining a heart to extend friendship to people like me. She endeavored to learn Arabic, which was a bridge she built, not just between two languages, but between two worlds.

Our friendship blossomed. They say that curiosity is a form of caring, and Janet had curiosity by the truckload. She embodied the quote by Stephen R. Covey, "Seek first to understand, then to be understood." She defied conventional barriers and forged friendships in a mosque—a place where most Catholics and Christians would be afraid to visit. Janet's presence at the mosque, where she sat and engaged with us at various events, was a beacon of inclusivity and kindness. While she did not worship the God that we did, she did not feel like an outsider.

I lent my knowledge of Arabic to her, while she, in turn, became a guide for me in navigating the challenges of English. We had meals in her home, shared laughs, and time together. Her initiative was inspiring. In a time of personal transition, it was as if the divine had placed people like Janet in my path, illuminating my journey with the light of unexpected friendships that bridged worlds and warmed hearts. God had orchestrated the right people at the right time to sustain me in an hour of loneliness.

I was excited to be diving into campus life and broadening my horizons through people like Janet. Similar to LSU, I made it a point to participate in various clubs and events beyond the classroom. One such gathering would serve to open my eyes and challenge much of the dogma I had been exposed to from childhood.

* * *

The air is filled with the static hum and intermittent crackle of the radio as it struggles to find a clear signal. Amidst the white noise, as if emerging from a distant world, the crackling subsides, giving way to the clear, articulate voice of an Iranian radio host. The voice, speaking first in Farsi, recounts current events from around the world. Then, almost as a shadow to the Farsi speaker, a translation into Arabic unfolds, which I could understand as a child.

Because Shia Muslims, like my family, maintain loyalty to Iran and not the Sunni-based Saudi government, we consistently listened to Iranian radio growing up with live translation into our native Arabic. I distinctly recall the rhetoric that came through the airwaves. Generally, the broadcaster would talk about how Israel was the source of pain in the world and the cause for any downturn in the Middle Eastern economy. They were always linking Israel and the United States as the two guilty perpetrators of trouble around the world. The vitriol seemed like an obsession to them.

"Death to America," would be shouted by the broadcaster while countless listeners around the Middle East nodded in agreement.[13] I was being indoctrinated with anti-American and anti-Israeli sentiment from the start. In fact, when my mother became particularly angry and wanted to insult me, she would say, "You daughter of a Jew!" | "يا بنت اليهودية"

So that makes you the Jew? I would think to myself.

These hatreds were not merely imported from Iran but were homegrown in Saudi as well. From Mecca, during the call to prayer, a broadcast would come from the main mosque with prayers that said, "Oh Allah, we pray that Allah will destroy the Jews and the Americans. Amen... disperse them, make their women widows and make their children orphans...Amen." "اللهم عليك باليهود والأمريكان اللهم ....آمين

"شتت شملهم ... آمين ، اللهم يتم أطفالهم ورمل نسائهم ......آمين

My response, even then as a small child, was that I despised this kind of speech. I was taught to hate Israel, but I could not. It simply was not in me to do so. I had never met

13. أمريكا أمريكا الموت لأمريكا، عدو الشعوب مثيرة الحروب.
Translation: "America, America death to America, the enemy of the nations, and warmonger of wars." The "Death to America" slogan originated in Iran during the Islamic Revolution.

a Jew; how could I hate them? I had no American friends; how could I wish death upon them? I held this quiet resistance to Islamic intolerance throughout my early life. Once I was finally in America, I had the chance to push back even more when I was invited to a club at Chico State called *The Children of Abraham Coalition*.

Having never met a Jewish person, but hearing much about them my entire life, I was curious to do so. The club, at its core, sought to foster respect and understanding amongst the three major monotheistic faiths that stem from their shared patriarch, Abraham. Judaism, Christianity, and Islam have been rife with conflict throughout history, so the idea that the divide could be bridged and healthy interfaith dialogue could happen seemed incredible. It was something that simply could never and would never happen back home.

Their goal as an organization was to encourage mutual respect, understanding, to rally around shared values, and to dispel myths. For me, that was exactly what happened. Before the first meeting, I did not know what to expect. Bear in mind, I had been told things like, "The Jews have the devil's eyes," for most of my life. While I did not buy into the hatred, it was still an area of hesitation for me. I was insatiably curious and anxious to get to the meeting.

When the day came, I walked into the hall on campus where the gathering was held. Refreshments and snacks sat on a table in the corner while people mingled and chatted around the room. I noted hijabs, yamikas, as well as standard Western attire. There was no yelling, shouting, or unrest of any kind. When I was able to meet some of the Jewish people in the room, I was delighted to see that they lacked "the eyes of devils" and were perfectly kind, wonderful people. While asking and answering questions, smiling and exchanging conversation, I wondered, *What would people in Saudi think of me standing here peacefully amongst Jews and Christians?*

I found that I felt safer talking to men in the States, compared with Saudi men back home. They were open to ideas and less set in their ways. They gave more value to the words spoken by women, and I felt I had a seat at the table, so to speak. I wound up attending *The Children of Abraham* gathering on multiple occasions, and with each visit, I sensed a shift occurring in my perceptions and worldview. Somewhere inside me, I felt the grip of former ideas being loosened as my new experience was not in agreement with my past teaching.

The Quran certainly taught that the people of these faith groups were my sworn enemies. As a devout Muslim, I had to acknowledge this as true. Yet I was presented with a glaring problem: I knew it was *not* true. I wanted no war with them. I longed to see them flourish as humans, and the thought of their downfall brought me no joy.

In this, I was feeling the early pangs of cognitive dissonance—the stress of holding two opposing beliefs at once.

This sort of angst cannot be sustained long term, and within me, I felt a change was coming, or perhaps, had already begun. As my perceptions changed, so did my behavior. For instance, upon moving to the U.S., finding suitable food proved to be troublesome. My younger brother had moved to Chico two years after I arrived in the States on the same scholarship. Every month, he and I would embark on a two-hour drive to Sacramento to buy halal meat from a Muslim market. Each trip felt like a pilgrimage that reaffirmed our commitment to the Islamic practices. However, as time went by, the once bearable sacrifice of this monthly ritual began to weigh heavily on me. The inconvenience of the long drives and the hours spent on the road started to loom larger with each trip.

The decision to stop eating halal meat was not sudden. It evolved from a slow realization, a series of compromises that I reluctantly made in the face of practical challenges. It was a significant shift, not just in my diet, but in how I viewed my place between two worlds.

During that season, I picked up a side job for the school as a tutor, helping non-Arabic students to learn Arabic. The university needed the help, I liked the work, and $30 per hour meant extra shopping money for me. In Saudi, there is no "teenage job" for girls like in the States, so this was my first experience in any sort of employment. The tutor position came about because there were Americans in the process of converting to Islam, and part of that entry involves reading passages from the Quran in Arabic, with proper Arabic pronunciation.

One young American lady asked me, "Can I still go to heaven if I don't pronounce the passage properly?"

"Just do it in English," I told her.

"No. The Imam told me it has to be in Arabic with correct pronunciation."

I worked with her, yet the guttural language was too difficult for her to grasp. *Why does it have to be in Arabic?* I wondered. She wasn't pronouncing it correctly anyway. Why couldn't she read a translation?

Because the Quran was "revealed" in Arabic, it must be received in Arabic. In fact, prayers in other languages and recitations of the Quran in anything other than Arabic are simply not accepted by Allah. To me, this simply did not follow logically. If a person wanted to be included in the faith and desired to adhere to Islamic customs, but simply struggled with pronunciation, why should they be bound for hell?

I called my mom and ranted, "Mom, these people are trying their best and praying, but can't pronounce these passages correctly. Why should they be excluded from Islam? That sounds like the rule of a mean god to me."

"You're privileged, Sahar. You grew up knowing it, but they will just have to learn."

The Quran taught that Allah was a just God. Inside of me was a strong sense of justice that I had carried with me from childhood. Now, however, it seemed that Allah himself was violating *my* internal sense of justice. How could the God who gave me a sense of justice then *violate* that sense through these ruthless, arbitrary rules imposed on seekers of truth? I began seeing a cruelty in Allah's dealings with mankind that I simply could not ignore.

Even reflecting on my childhood, I noted perspectives that were so off base. I still remember the day 9/11 happened. I was just 16 years old at the time, and I can never forget the chilling moment when a male family member actually rejoiced in the tragedy, saying, "Death to America and their ideologies." That moment shook me to my core—a combination of shock, confusion, and a deep sense of shame that stayed with me for years. Children would wait for their mothers and fathers to come home from work that day, only to learn they would grow up without that parent. Why? Because of an Islamic ideology.

Growing up as a Shia Muslim, I was taught that by attacking America and Israel, we would bring about the Khilafah (Caliphate). In this belief, Shia Muslims were preparing the way for Al-Mahdi, the 12th Imam who had disappeared and would return at the end of times to bring peace on Earth. Jesus, too, was said to return and follow Al-Mahdi. These teachings had a profound impact on my worldview, but as I grew older, they began to feel increasingly difficult to reconcile with the reality I saw unfolding.

Many years later, I recall vividly the day during my first

year in the U.S. when my English class asked me to write an essay about 9/11. What seemed like a simple assignment at first ended up forcing me to confront something I hadn't fully processed. As I wrote, I found myself questioning my faith, my identity, and the connection between who I was as a Muslim and what had just unfolded in the world.

It was a painful moment. I felt an overwhelming sense of shame about being a Muslim, especially in the aftermath of such a horrific tragedy. At the time, I couldn't deny that the actions of the attackers seemed to be justified by the teachings of the Quran—that they believed they were following a call to kill the "infidels." But even in that painful moment, there was a quiet, conflicting thought deep inside me: I'm not *that kind* of Muslim. I believed in peace, in love, and I knew that wasn't the path I followed. Yet, the contradictions in the teachings of Islam left me struggling.

The Quran, as I understood it, seemed full of contradictions. Some verses spoke of peace, while others seemed to advocate violence. The inner tension between these extremes left me feeling lost and conflicted. To cope with this, I convinced myself that I was following the peaceful path of Islam—that I was embracing the love, mercy, and compassion that I believed should define my faith. It was my way of reconciling the peace I felt in my heart with the violent images I saw in the world around me.

Writing that essay on U.S. soil made me reflect deeply. We, as Muslims, often want to be educated by the West, yet we simultaneously consider them our enemies. The fact that they are so advanced in fields like education, science, and technology speaks volumes about who they are as a society. Their intellect, innovation, and the positive contributions they offer to the world stand in stark contrast to the victim mindset many Muslims have. Instead of looking inward to ask why we're struggling, there's often a tendency to blame others for our backwardness and loss of power. Yet, it was clear to me that real progress comes not from external blame, but from internal transformation—educating ourselves, cultivating intellect, and learning to contribute to the world in meaningful ways.

Muslims often found themselves on the ruins—remembering the great days of the Islamic conquests (الفتوحات الإسلامية), Al-Andalus, and the Ottoman Empire. There was a sense of longing for the glory days of Islam, a yearning to return to a time when we, as a people, were powerful and influential. But this feeling, while deeply ingrained, was also clouded by the contradictions I saw in my faith and the world around me.

The questions and doubts multiplied. At the same time, there were no other religions or worldviews that interested me as an alternative to Islam. At the same time, I could not help but see serious inconsistencies and contradictions within my Muslim faith. Charged with a sense of Western free thought, I adopted a critical eye toward the faith I had always known. I began to see how writers of the Quran had twisted history to their liking. It was taught that Abraham worshiped in Mecca, which is the location where he nearly sacrificed his son. They taught, unlike Christians and Jews, that Abraham brought Ishmael to the altar, not Isaac. Because of this, Mecca is the holiest site in all of Islam. The problem is, all records that predate the writing of the Quran point to the fact that Abraham never once stepped foot in Arabia.

It began to appear that the writers of the Quran had just forged Middle Eastern history and justified it by claiming it was a "divine revelation," wherein Allah set the record straight. I was uneasy with this idea. The Jewish people had been keeping records of the Middle East for over 2,000 years before Islam began. Christians had done the same for 600 years before Muhammad ever drew a breath on this earth. The origin of the faith that my life had been built upon began to seem rather suspicious.

Religion in pre-Islamic Arabia was a mixture of polytheism, Christianity, Judaism, and obscure Iranian religions. Collyridianism gained steam, which was a heretical version of Christianity that elevated Mary as a goddess to be worshiped. Sabianism, which was a version of astrology, was practiced along with gnostic movements like Manichaeism. In short, it was an area of the world marked by the confusion of a very messy religious landscape.

One man showed up to clear up this confusion. Muhammad was born in modern Mecca in the Quraysh tribe, a powerful merchant group. Orphaned before the age of six, he was raised by his grandfather and then by an uncle. He was known early on for being smart, strong, and wise. He eventually married a woman, 14 years his elder, a widow named Khadijah. He helped her in business, which she was quite successful in.

When he was 40, he began receiving supposed revelations from God through the angel Gabriel. These, of course, were recorded, and much later, after his death, the Quran came together as a book of his teachings. Strangely enough, it was a cousin of Muhammad's wife who first referred to him as a prophet and declared that God was giving him the final message. Through conquest, wars, fighting, and campaigns, Muhammad and his followers spread the message of Islam. Any Christians and Jews who remained in the area were required to convert, pay jizya (money as punishment), or be killed. Under Islamic law, if the money is not paid, the people are to be killed or enslaved. Now, nearly 1,500 years later, those of other faiths still find no hospitality in the region.

As I pored over the life of Muhammad, I saw the unreliability of what I was reading and what I was practicing. When he was alive, only his wives covered themselves (he wound up having 11 in total). His wives were quite beautiful, and he was jealous that they might be seen by others. As a result, he covered them, but he did not require his female followers to cover.

The Hadith[14] taught that if a woman does *not* cover, God will punish her according to the number of hairs she has on her head. It seemed to me that if the covering was so critical, Muhhamad would have talked about it, or surely there would have been a mention of this in the Quran. Instead, it was infused later in the Hadith and adopted by early followers. I became convinced that covering was just a cultural decision that had nothing to do with Islam or Allah's actual will.

When I looked around at my Muslim community, I saw women who were accustomed to doing as they were told, without question and without reading. That was not me. If I were going to do something as consequential as covering myself daily for all of my existence on earth, I needed to know the origin and source of the practice.

The scarf bothered me for practical reasons as well. I felt I needed sunlight and room to breathe. My hair was shedding—it was not healthy for my scalp to be covered for so long, devoid of vitamin D. Ultimately, I did not think the practice was required according to my faith. With theological and practical reasons backing me, in 2009, I made the

---

14. Hadīth refers to what most Muslims and the mainstream schools of Islamic thought believe to be a record of the words, actions, and the silent approval of the Islamic prophet Muhammad. The Quran is viewed as the authentic and faultless word of Allah, whereas the Hadith is a collection of narratives about the prophet Muhammad. Shia have their own Hadith (different from the Sunni Hadith). They read books and scripted prayers such as Hadith al-Kisa | حديث الكساء, Dua al-Tawassul | دعاء التوسل, Mafatih al-Jinan | مفاتيح الجنان, and Nahj al-Balāgha | نهج البلاغة, and so on.

decision to uncover myself. It was a choice I came to on my own, without any sort of outside compulsion. This was an internal conviction, not external coercion.

The first time I uncovered in public, I felt naked. I went to class wearing a Chico State baseball cap, and most of my peers did not know who I was. I had a feminist teacher who noticed the change immediately. Thrilled with my newfound freedom, she suggested I sleep around as well. Apparently, removing a hijab was a baby step to promiscuity in her mind.

As I adjusted to the change, I found support in my brother. "I don't blame you," he said, "People treat *me* differently when I'm with you. They avoid me when we walk together. But when I'm alone, people have no problem approaching me. They're more open and friendly. I can't imagine how alienating it must be for you."

My mother did not receive it so kindly. She fumed with anger and expressed her dissatisfaction in no uncertain terms. She felt as though I was jumping onto the slippery slope of becoming a Westerner and losing my roots and values. Because my brother was technically responsible for me as a male figure in the country, she was also mad at him for permitting this. When she later came to the States on a summer visit, she better understood my decision, realizing that the aim of the hijab, to draw attention away from yourself, actually did the opposite in the West and made a lady stand out more.

My decision-making process is a long, slow, and thoughtful one. Once I have made up my mind and become fully convinced, I move on from thinking to *acting*. When the decision is made, the decision is made, and I do not go back under any circumstances. The day I took off the covering was final, and I never did so again. The very next day, my sister, who was also in the States by that time, took hers off as well.

The feeling of nakedness in public eventually subsided, and Western attire became my new normal. I was not exposed but *unveiled*. This opened a door to self-discovery in a new way. I had grown up in a faith that barely allowed me to know God, much less myself. After a few years in America, I began taking personality tests to better understand *myself.* For a time, while my brother was living in Chico, we would talk, compare experiences, and discuss all things life and faith. It seemed that I was entering a new season of clarity as I looked beyond life after school. My final stretch of classes at Chico was hard and stressful. I loaded my schedule with extra credit hours to finish by my original graduation date, allowing for major changes.

I felt accomplished as graduation day approached. Many Saudi students, men especially, came on the scholarship to have fun. They wrestled with culture shock, and because their female professors were not covered, male Saudi students often did not respect them and even considered them promiscuous. Meanwhile, they would spend their government money on trips to Vegas and parties. When the Saudi government discovered these young men had bad academic scores, they were all brought back, and their scholarships were canceled.

These days, the restrictions on that scholarship have tightened, and students are required to sign a form stating that if they do not pass the classes, they have to pay the tuition money back. For me, other than uncovering and becoming a skeptic of my own faith, I had maintained good standing with Saudi requirements while studying abroad. I kept my academic honor and fought for good marks.

During my time in college, my doubt in Islam was at a fever pitch. But something else happened: I kept meeting many Christ-followers on campus. In classrooms, at gatherings, or in common places, I would meet believers in Jesus who would share the Bible or answer my questions about Jesus and Christianity. I was exposed to the depths of the Christian faith and even visited an American and Arabic Christian church. While I did not drop everything to run and get baptized, my college experience definitely began to open me up to things I never would have considered before.

Beyond rethinking my faith, I was rethinking my future. As my academic career came to a close, I started to consider what work would look like in the years to come. In the Spring of 2011, I walked the stage and was handed my diploma, displaying my new Bachelor's degree, which was a promise of a better future. During my season in California, a different document had also been handed to me. It was a leatherbound book, given by a stranger on campus a few months after arriving in Chico, which also held a promise of a better future, whether I knew it or not at the time. I looked at it, and on the cover were the words "Holy Bible" | الكتاب المقدس.

CHAPTER SEVEN

Testing the Water

And sinking deep!

"There are far, far better things ahead than any we leave behind."
—C.S. Lewis

She did not just hand me the Bible but also uttered the words, "Jesus loves you." I knew Christians talked a lot about love and forgiveness, so I did not stagger backwards with a life-changing revelation, nor did I fall to my knees in repentance. To me, the notion of love from God seemed silly. In our culture, *stated* love is not impressive, but greater emphasis is given to *actions*. At the time, I had not come to understand the actions that gave evidence to her words.

In Arabic, we use terms of endearment with those we love, and we give affectionate titles, such as "Habibi/Habibti حبيبي / حبيبتي," which literally means "my love." But the words, "I love you," do not carry the weight they do in the West. I walked away thinking, *Why would a prophet love me? Chris-*

tians are crazy. I certainly was not convinced of a new way of life, but at least these seeds planted were more positive compared with the aggressive street preaching I had seen on campus before.

I opened the Bible out of curiosity and read a story in which Jesus walked past a fig tree and proceeded to curse it, saying, "You will never bear fruit!" *Wow,* I thought. *This Jesus is crazy. Was he in a bad mood? Did he need a nap?* Of course, I was not aware of the context, symbolism of fruitfulness, Israel, and the scope of the Gospel as a whole. I just thought it seemed strange and neurotic.

By the time my days at Chico came to a close, I had come to learn that Christians were not my sworn enemies after all, though I was far from being "born again" myself. My skepticism toward Islam was at an all-time high, and the thought of going back to a fully covered life in Saudi put a pit in my stomach. I decided to delay the return by working for a year before coming back to university for a master's degree.

Aside from tutoring on campus, I had no past employment, so naturally I was thrilled to add some experience to my resume. I thought of my dad often. Here I was at 27, graduated, and making a start of my own, which was not uncommon for Saudis, whereas he was thrown into the workforce at 17 with siblings and a mother to care for. I had his courage and drive to draw on as I made yet another move to another state to begin a career.

An oil company in Boulder, Colorado needed an intern for a three-month contract. The idea was that I would be hired full-time after that quarter as an intern. The company worked with clients in Saudi and Kuwait, yet had never hired someone from the Middle East. As an insider, I consulted with them about culture, advising them in their interactions with clients while also working on their customer relationship management.

I was surrounded by engineers who would travel to and from the Middle East, so the office was often empty, leaving me with nothing to do. I read books and took the bus home, passing the time in my cozy apartment nestled in the snowy Rocky Mountain landscape. The snow-capped horizon was sublime, though most of my time was spent inside, avoiding the brutally cold winter weather.

I liked my job overall, but the rigid nine-to-five schedule was a challenge. Living under such extreme control for most of my life had instilled in me a deep need for freedom and flexibility. Even to this day, at a conference or seminar, my first move is to look at the schedule and determine which session I'm going to skip. Why? Because it simply is not in me to adhere to a rigid outline. Growing up under oppression can have an interesting impact on an individual's habits.

I did not know it at the time, but Boulder is known for being a rather atheistic and sometimes New Age city. Despite this, it seemed that everywhere I went, I was encountering Christians. Early on, I caught wind of a gathering of international students and workers at a hub near my place. With a non-existent social life, I figured it wouldn't hurt to go and mingle. There I met a girl from Turkey, Ibru, who became somewhat of a friend, at least for the time being. She had been in the States for a while and, like me, had wound up in Boulder for work. Unlike me, however, she had left the Muslim faith and became a Christian. She was quite transparent on that subject from the start.

Something curious happened when she would speak of her Jesus: I saw light in her face. In fact, she introduced me to her friend group, many of whom were former Muslims, and they all seemed to glow with peace and excitement when speaking of Christ and heaven. The transformation was evident in their countenance. We would have dinner together occasionally, and I observed a stark difference between them and me. Muslims are terrified of the afterlife, but these people seemed to lean into the topic as if speaking of an exciting new restaurant. From where did they derive such hope?

More than once, they invited me to their home group where they would pray, read, and study the Bible together. I successfully maintained my stubborn walls for weeks, politely turning down the invitation. Finally, after over two months, I acquiesced and decided to attend. There were about nine of us in total, gathered in a small living room, each with a Bible in hand.

I looked around the room and saw people who loved one another. It seemed as if they were *one*, despite coming from various nations, backgrounds, and walks of life. I thought of my own faith and wished that Muslims would gather for a Quran study like this. Then again, Muslims argue so much that it wouldn't be a peaceful gathering anyway.

As the study was underway, the group began discussing the Apostle Paul and his teachings. Apparently, he had written much of the New Testament and seemed to be an important figure for these people. The lady who had invited me lent me a Bible for the time being that had both Arabic and English translations in it. As they read Scripture, I looked for the book of Paul, which was nowhere to be found.

As I searched, my eyes fell upon a passage in Matthew 22, where Jesus is being questioned about marriage and heaven. The Sadducees, who were skeptical of life after death, asked Jesus whose wife a widow would be since she had many husbands on earth. I was quite curious to hear the reply of Jesus, "But Jesus answered them, 'You are wrong, because you know neither the Scriptures nor the power of God. For in the resurrection they neither marry nor are given in marriage, but are like angels in heaven'" (Matthew 22:29-30).

This arrested me. In Islam, heaven is all about sex. One only needs to look at the doctrine of Muslim men being rewarded with 72 virgins to see this. To me, hell certainly sounded awful, but heaven itself did not sound much better. It seemed like an eternal continuation of the oppression of women on earth. Yet here in this Scripture, Jesus was describing a heaven that had no emphasis on sex or marriage at all. *Wow,* I thought. *This is the heaven I want.* I found it to be incredible and re-read it multiple times, experiencing fresh waves of fascination with each pass through.

I went home and opened the Bible with a cautious curiosity. Beginning in Matthew, I made my way through the life and teachings of Jesus. I noted the woman with the issue of blood. Surely she was breaking the rules by being out and about in such a state. Jesus met her, not with a rebuke, but with tender words and a miracle, lovingly calling her "daughter" as she went in peace, fully healed. In the gospel of John, I saw the woman at the well, who had a shaky history with men. Jesus did not condemn her to hell or give her the cold shoulder like one might expect. Instead, he engaged in a dialogue and pointed her toward the possibilities of eternal life. She was shocked that a Jew would speak to her, a Samaritan. I was stunned that a prophet would give the time of day to a woman with a past like hers.

Then, I came to the story of the woman caught in adultery. She was found in the act and dragged into the streets for justice. Pharisees surrounded her with stones in hand, ready to execute her for her crime. In her defense, Jesus gave the crowd an ultimatum: "He who is without sin, throw the first stone" (see John 8:7). Rocks hit the ground one by one, as they all realized they had no moral authority to carry out the judgment. Jesus then turned to the woman and asked, "Where are your accusers?" They had left. "I do not condemn you," he said. "Go and sin no more" (see John 8:10-11).

Had this scene unfolded in the Quran, I could not help but feel that Muhammad would have had a stone in hand. His regard for the well-being of women was non-existent. In Jesus, however, I found an advocate and a man who understood and met women right where they were. I could not deny that these stories were touching me deeply, and I felt that Jesus had a goal of empowering women. All I had known was a culture that treated women as a means to an end. It is understood that men and women are different in personality and biology, yet at the heart of Islam is the notion that men and women are different in *value*.

I did not see this same sort of assessment in the life of Jesus. From big issues to small ones, I observed the second-rate treatment of women as a deeply ingrained flaw in Middle Eastern culture. For instance, after moving to the U.S., I had asked my mother for help getting a car, which was always denied year after year. Of course, just months after moving to America, she provided one for my brother. Even in the sprawling USA, with minimal public transportation, a car was just something a woman did not need in her view.

In these recollections, I found myself torn. The culture and theology that I had always known, Islam, seemed to produce nothing but oppression. The theology that I disliked, Christianity, seemed to produce freedom, empowerment, and transformation. Every time I saw a former Muslim talking about Christianity, they honed in on one thing specifically: personal transformation. It was not as though they simply gained a new way of thinking or a novel belief structure, but their attitudes, lifestyle, outlook, and behavior as a whole seemed to undergo great and measurable *change*. Change is hard to come by, and it is difficult to fake, yet all around me were people who clearly had experienced it.

I was being slowly convinced, and I didn't want to be. Even during my time at Chico, my French Tutor, "Koala" from Burkina Faso, would not stop sharing the gospel with me. Person by person, place by place, I was being pursued. I was finding truth in what these Christians said, but did not want to be persuaded. I felt that if I stayed in their group, I would become a Christian, which was the last thing I wanted. There is a scene in the book of Acts where Agrippa says to the Apostle Paul, "You almost persuade me to become a Christian." I related to Agrippa in that season of my life. It was a fearful thing to become a Christian, as it had massive cultural implications. In fact, a Christian Saudi sounded like a contradiction. Islam is not merely a way of believing but a national identity.

With the Bible open, everything in me wanted this heaven that Jesus spoke of. I wanted my God to treat me as Jesus treated women, but my questions and skepticism toward Christianity kept me away. *How can God be a man? Why would he need to die?* I would close the Bible and open the Quran to compare texts. There, I read a chapter about Jesus and Mary, which described Him merely as a "prophet" but not God.

Going back to the Bible, I read further as Jesus alluded to Himself as God, and I finally closed it, pushing it away and uttering the words, "Istaghfur Allah | استغفر الله" meaning, "God forbid this." From there, I became very religious about Islam. I tried with extra fervor to be a good, devout Muslim, kicking back against the Christian influence in Boulder.

During that season, I recall talking to Christians who attended an Arabic church and questioning them. "I am a Muslim," I would say, "and I will die a Muslim. I'm just here to learn. I don't need persuasion, don't try to convince me, just answer my questions if I have any." They respectfully answered everything I threw at them.

I would debate and push back. One Turkish Christian woman in Boulder eventually said to me, "If what you believe is true, then you pray for me to go back to Islam. I'll pray for you to become a Christian. Let's see whose God wins."

The gauntlet was officially thrown down. The problem is, the more I read the Quran, the more I struggled to accept it as true. Despite my reactionary fit of Islamic zeal, internally, my skepticism grew by the day. I decided at the end of my three-month internship that I needed to turn down a full-time position in Boulder and leave that environment. I also did not want to return to Chico and felt a fresh start was in order. I needed me, my thoughts, and neutral ground to search. Deep inside, I felt I would eventually start something on my own, whether an international business or something in fashion that linked the Middle East and the U.S.

In the meantime, however, I found a job with flexibility doing software sales in San Jose. I eased into the California climate again and continued my internal search. What began as an unemotional, neutral investigation into my faith ended in the realization that to be a Muslim, you must believe what Muslims believe. Yet, in the bustling streets of San Jose, amidst the tech boom and the melting pot of cultures and religions, I found myself drifting further from the certainties I had grown up with. The job that brought me here was a fun new challenge, but the journey within me was what consumed me the most and truly marked this period of my life.

The issue was not Islam versus Christianity, Islam versus Hinduism, or Islam versus anything else. I was not comparing the Quran and the Bhagavad Gita. The true contest was Islam versus *me*. I would turn to the Quran | القرآن with a genuine desire to connect with my roots, to find the peace promised within its pages. But with every verse and Hadith | الحديث, instead of finding clarity, I encountered more questions. Questions about justice, about women, about Muhammad, violence, and about the hate Islam promotes toward anyone who does not think like them or dares to question their theology. It wasn't a defiant rejection but a gradual realization. The values and principles I admired personally, like compassion, equality, and the relentless pursuit of knowledge, seemed at odds with the text I was presented with.

This dissonance led me down a path I had not anticipated when I walked off the plane in Baton Rouge those years earlier, but here I was. The sun would set over the Santa Cruz mountains, and I would be alone in the quiet of my apartment to reflect, think, and suffer.

Ultimately, it wasn't a dramatic moment of renunciation but a firm acceptance of the fact that I was no longer a Muslim. It was not due to resentment toward my culture or a knee-jerk desire to rebel. I simply saw one thing lacking in the faith I had always known: *truth*. My decision was slow but final; the Islamic faith was no longer my own. In a sense, it didn't even feel like *my* decision. I had simply placed myself in a search for truth and had gotten swept away in the tide. Like a flying trapeze artist, I had let go of one bar and was now suspended in midair, looking for the next one to grab—if there was one at all.

* * *

Leaving Islam was more than a change of opinion; it was the

removal of an identity. My deconstruction was an affront to my culture, national heritage, and family history, which meant the stakes were high. I've often found that my decisions are like oak trees. The research, rationale, and consideration may have started as a small acorn, but slowly over time grows into something strong and immovable. When I'm convinced of something, my instinct is to be outspoken about it. In this case, I knew Islam was an enormous pool of deception, and that was something I could not stay silent on. It was with this realization that I came to terms with the fact that I could not return to Saudi Arabia. How dare I go back and live like a Muslim, shrouded and oppressed, when I was not one?

It was clear, I needed to stay in the USA.

I applied for asylum shortly after. The woman who interviewed me for the case wore a pleasant smile the whole time, eventually telling me that her own case looked just like mine. I did one interview and later mailed further information, translating my permission card[15] from Arabic and scrounging together endless documents. Everything happened fast, like an escape in the night. Once submitted, it was time to wait for the green card, with travel being forbidden—which was no problem, as I didn't want to travel on a Saudi passport anyway.

Coming to the end of Islam was coming to the start of

---

15. We call it in Arabic "تصريح خروج" which means Exit permit.

the unknown. I settled into my search in San Jose by attending two gatherings each week. One was at a standard Christian megachurch in the area. The music was nice, and their messages were simple but profound. Each Sunday, they invited people to accept Jesus, often by coming down to the front of the church. I quietly sat on the second-floor balcony, looked down, and vowed to never do such a thing. I was simply curious, not a Christ follower in the making.

I must admit, I *loved* their Bible studies. Beforehand, I asked them, "I'm not a Christian, but can I still attend?"

"Sure thing," I was told.

In the group, they studied the Trinity. As a former Muslim, this was a sticking point for me. How could God be *one* but still exist as Father, Son, and Holy Spirit? I learned much from them on the topic, but still had questions. I noticed that they were comfortable with saying things like, "The Trinity is a mystery. We don't know how it works exactly, we just know that God is three-in-one."

Hearing a Christian say, "I don't know," was extremely refreshing to me. In Islam, the Imams claimed to know everything, having all of the answers scripted and memorized. They would share things with absolute confidence and then say, "God knows best!" | الله أعلم! Yet here I found Christians who were comfortable with the unknowns. It felt real and authentic. "We don't know everything," they would say, "if we did, we would be God."

The other weekly gathering was at an Arabic Christian

church that met an hour outside of San Jose for Sunday night services. I had heard about it through mutual friends and made the drive. The community there was close-knit and smaller, naturally. The mother of the pastor would occasionally invite me to stay at her place in order to avoid the late-night drive, which meant I had the opportunity to ask questions in bulk.

I had endless questions for her about the person of Jesus. "I want to follow him as a prophet," I would say, "but not as God." She would talk through Christ's divinity and nature. This, of course, led to even more questions. *How can God be known?* In my upbringing, God was either mad or merciful, which meant we walked on eggshells. Other than this polarity, we know nothing of God's actual character traits. However, in the Bible, I saw that God laughs, He cries, He rejoices, and He grieves. He is not without feelings and emotions.

I saw that people talked to God as though they were talking to their dad. The intimacy of prayer in the Christian life blew my mind. I was awakened to the complex character of God and the notion that He is personal, knowable, relatable. Personal knowledge of God just did not exist in Muslim community—God was far away, and your confidence in him was even further. The fear of punishment ran rampant in Islam, but here in Christian communities, believers lived like they were accepted, children of God. It was the common disposition of Christians everywhere I looked. I even attended an Iranian church made up of former Shia Muslims and saw that their joy in God was noticeable. I would attend their services and don headphones that offered live translation of the sermon from Farsi to English. The last time I had experienced this was Iranian radio spewing vitriol toward Israel and America. Now, though, I was hearing a better message.

Still, my many questions persisted. At a picnic with this particular church, I recall asking, "If there is only one God, why do people experience miracles in other faiths?"

A woman across the table answered, "Well, there is only one true God, and He is *all*-powerful. Satan has power, too, though, and he deceives people. He can work false miracles. Because he is the root of sickness, he can take away the affliction when people pray to a false god. It reinforces their faith in a false idea and keeps them deceived."

The Bible *did* suggest that Satan was cunning and smart, and the answer felt cogent, sticking with me to this day. The truth is, I was not just learning a new concept of God but a new concept of the demonic, too. Growing up, I heard a lot about demons and encountered them firsthand, but this was no cause for concern, as demons could be good or bad. I hoped we had the good ones, of course. The Christian view was unique in that it taught that the devil walked about like a roaring lion, which scared me. I began to consider the possibility that I had grown up with evil spirits that I had simply shrugged off as "the good ones" that were there to protect me.

Beyond bouncing around diverse churches to grill the pastors and congregants with questions, I also went straight to the source. I would open the Bible and read, not necessarily for enlightenment, but to find mistakes. When I was in Colorado, Ibru told me about her encounter with the Bible. "My sister began reading the Bible," she told me, "and wound up giving her life to Jesus. I felt like she was crazy, but I couldn't help but notice the change in her. A kindness and a love seemed to overtake her. She invited me to church, and I went in order to make fun of Christians. Something was pulling on my heart, though, and I decided to go home, sit down, and read the Bible."

From there, she explained that in one single sitting, for hours and hours and hours, she read the entire Bible from Genesis to Revelation. Her goal was simply to be open and available to the truth. As she closed the final Scripture of the final book, she bowed her head and said, "I believe." At that moment, she became a follower of Jesus.

This was a powerful story and realization for me. Personally, I would just read bits and pieces of the Bible in order to better argue against it. I wanted to find fault, but she wanted to find truth. I wanted to win a debate, but she wanted to be won by God.

It was during that season that I reached out to a Christian friend from Chico to ask more questions about the Bible. She replied, "You have asked me these questions before, and I've given you all the answers I know to be true. Here's the thing, I grew up in a Christian home and have known this truth from childhood...I don't know how else to answer you. I believe you need to meet with someone who was a Muslim and became a follower of Jesus."

From there, she recommended that I connect with a specific man who had a Muslim background. I knew almost nothing about him, other than the fact that he had an Arabic name, and that I *really* needed to hear his story. With arrangements in place, I made the trip to see him.

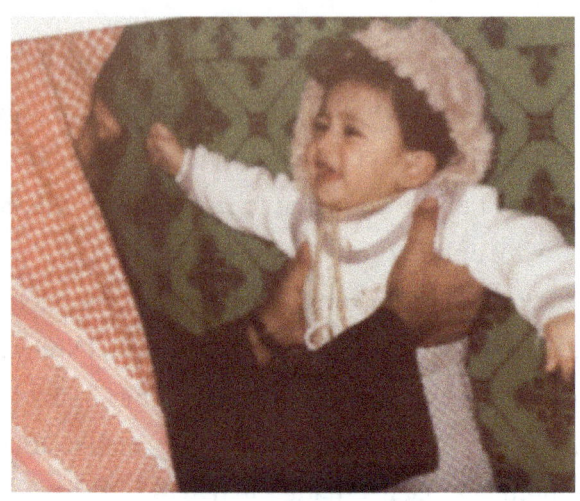

With my dad on a camping trip in the Saudi Desert, safe, and surrounded by his love. Alkhafji City, KSA.

Under my earthly Father's garment, it reminds me of sukkout (סוכות), where we sit under our heavenly Father's covering. Alkhafji City, KSA.

Pasta nights at home in Alkhafji. Pure childhood joy. Alkhafji City, KSA.

Caught wearing Mama's winter hat—shy, sweet, and a little embarrassed. Alkhafji City, KSA.

Sitting in peace on my parents' bed, dreaming beyond the walls.
Alkhafji City, KSA.

In Mama's lap, hugged by sisters. Warmth that lasts a lifetime.
Alkhafji City, KSA.

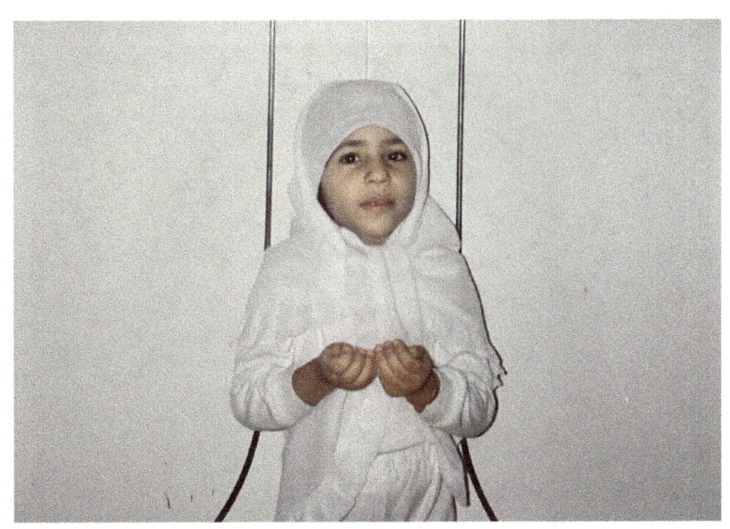

Praying to God. I know now—He truly heard me.
Alkhafji City, KSA.

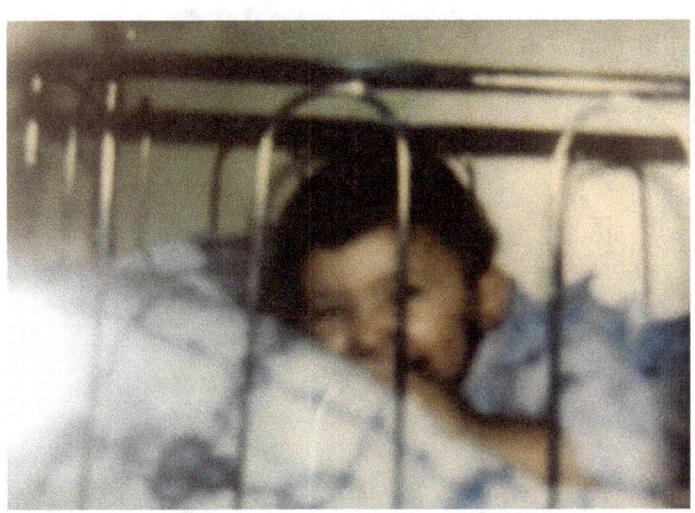

The joy of being alive. Bedtime bliss in Alkhafji City, KSA.

Another camping desert adventure with family. Where the coastal sands meet timeless stories. Alkhafji City, KSA.

I stole Mama's scissors... and cut my bangs. Not bad, huh? Alkhafji City, KSA.

With Grandpa and my sister. Generations of love.
Al-Qatif City, KSA.

Ready for school with my sister. Al-Qatif mornings.
Al-Qatif City, KSA.

Teenage years in Al-Qatif. A dreamer in a confined world. Al-Qatif City, KSA.

Saudi summers: hot, quiet, and boring, but I held onto hope.

My sister's wedding day—"Yom Al-Hinna | يوم الحنة."
Tradition, color, joy.

Umrah 2005. My face says it all—something stirred inside me.

San Francisco visit after finals. Freedom, wonder, and salty air.
Chico, CA, USA.

Leaving Saudi again for California. Bittersweet goodbyes. 2010.

College years in Chico. Laughter, growth, and furry friends. Chico, CA, USA.

Graduation season, 2012. From Chico into the unknown. Summer of 2012. Chico, CA, USA.

July 22, 2012. I met Jesus. Couldn't put His Word down.
San Jose, CA, USA.

Unveiling Beauty launched! A dream born. Irvine, California.
August, 2016.

I became an American! OKC, 2022. Let freedom ring!
OKC, Oklahoma, May, 2022.

Longing for home. I prayed I'd see them again soon.
Dallas, TX, 2022.

First trip with my U.S. passport.
Destiny begins: Nazareth, Israel, 2022.

Christmas in Nazareth, Israel 2022.

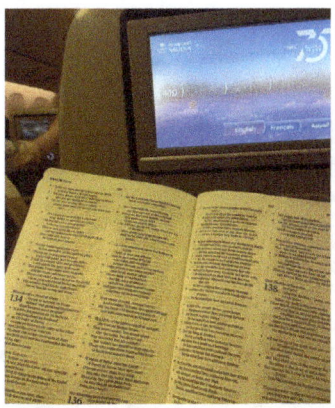

I returned to Saudi after 14 years of being away! Reading my Bible on a Saudi flight. A miracle in motion. March, 2023.

Landed on Founding Day. Hotel welcomed me with cake and the flag. Jeddah, KSA.

Prayers answered. Alkobar, KSA, 2023.

A new Saudi I never knew. Hair uncovered, heart open.
Al-Riyadh, Saudi Arabia, 2023.

Israel, 2024. Post-October 7th.
Tel Aviv to Jerusalem—my heart is here.

Walking the ancient streets of Jerusalem, filled with wonder and
fascination. Jerusalem, Israel, 2024.

Visiting LSU after 18 years. I'm no longer the girl I was. 2005.
Baton Rouge, Louisiana, USA.

CHAPTER EIGHT

Meeting Nabeel

Finding Jesus

"Truth silences falsehood."

—NABEEL QURESHI

Nabeel Qureshi was a promising Muslim student on the debate team while studying at Old Dominion in Norfolk, Virginia. Being on the debate team meant traveling for events and spending time with fellow debaters. During one competition, while the rest of the team went out drinking and partying the night before the debate, Nabeel stayed back. One other individual stayed back as well, a Christian named David. During the course of the night, David pulled out his Bible and began reading. Nabeel, who was sitting across the room, saw this and thought, *Alright, a chance to take down another Christian.*

"David, you realize that book is corrupt?" Nabeel began.

"Do share," David replied.

"Jesus spoke Aramaic. The early church spoke Hebrew. The New Testament was written in Greek. Plus, the churches used the Latin Vulgate for 1,000 years before it was translated into German and from there, English. You can't trust a document that's been translated and changed so many times."

Nabeel had a history of taking down Christians, often knowing the New Testament better than they themselves did. While he expected David to cave under scrutiny like the many Christians he encountered in the past, this was anything but the case.

In reply, David said, "Actually, we have in our possession today over 5,500 Greek New Testament manuscripts and can construct the entire New Testament from them. If that's not enough, we have over 10,000 Latin New Testament manuscripts. Even if we did not have those, we still have 8,000 Coptic Syriac New Testament manuscripts. Not enough? There are over 36,000 fragments and quotations of original manuscripts as well. From all this, we can easily piece together the original New Testament and verify that it has *not* been corrupted through time and translation. Our modern English versions are accurate."

"David, you're making this stuff up."

"Try me."

This began a rich and lasting friendship where the two took classes together, ate meals together, argued, debated, and studied their respective faiths. Nabeel was a devout Muslim apologist, and for years, he and David argued for their sides of the faith. In a sense, Nabeel had no choice in the matter. His grandparents were Islamic missionaries to

Indonesia and Uganda, dedicated preachers of Islam. He came from a long line of Muslim missionaries, and his father and mother were careful to set him up to continue the legacy.

Nabeel's parents had come to the United States in the mid-seventies in search of opportunity. His father landed in the USA on the day Elvis Presley died and, upon exiting the plane, noticed a newspaper with a giant headline stating, "The King is Dead." *Oh wow,* he thought. *I have a lot to learn. I thought America was a democracy.*

Shortly after, his father joined the U.S. Navy, and they planted their roots as a proud Muslim-American family. During Nabeel's upbringing, his mother would say, "Nabeel, you are an ambassador for Islam. If someone shares Christianity with you, share Islam in reply."

Before he even learned to speak and read English, he had already learned to read the Quran in Arabic. He held fond memories of childhood observance of feasts and ritualistic Islamic prayers. He learned arguments against the New Testament and the Christian view of Jesus and became a combative and fervent defender of Islam. From high school to college, Christians would crumble under his arguments. This made his encounter with David surprising and refreshing—he finally had a sparring partner.

Because their debates were housed in the context of an authentic friendship, the impact was different. Nabeel recounts, "I knew that David would take a bullet for me as my friend. This meant that when he tore down my faith and argued for Christianity...he was not doing it to be mean or to win an argument, but because he loved me."

At Nabeel's request, David decided to objectively investigate Islam, reading the Quran, the Hadith, and early sources like *Ibn Ishaq's Life of Muhammad,* and the *History of the Prophets* and *Kings* by Al-Tabari. It was a years-long deep dive, and David eventually concluded that the Quran and Muhammad's example not only *described* violence in the past (as in the Bible), but also *commanded* ongoing violence (unlike the Bible). This did two things: First, David recognized a call upon his life to argue on behalf of the Christian faith and to engage with Muslims specifically as an apologist. Second, Nabeel took up the same challenge and went about a multi-year deep dive into Christian teachings.

The two would regroup and hash out their findings. David argued that Christians were indeed monotheistic. Nabeel would argue that if you believe in the Trinity, you believe in three gods, not one. After all, Islam started when Muhammad pioneered the largely polytheistic Middle East with a message of monotheism—a point that Muslims remain very proud of. David would talk about the resurrection of Christ, and Nabeel would discuss the five pillars of Islam.

During Nabeel's search, he found the manuscript evidence to be more than compelling and determined that the New Testament was accurate. In other words, what is writ-

ten in modern Bibles about Jesus is exactly how it was recorded in the first century. This, of course, was not enough
for Nabeel. He still needed to verify a few things.

First, he needed to see evidence that Jesus claimed to
be God. Second, he required proof that Jesus died upon a
cross, and third, Nabeel had to know if the resurrection of
Jesus actually occurred. For him, it all hinged on these three
points of dispute. These questions came from the New Testament writer, Paul, specifically his note about salvation in
Romans 10:9, "...because, if you confess with your mouth
that Jesus is Lord and believe in your heart that God raised
him from the dead, you will be saved."

By this point in their friendship, it was clear that David
was not at all convinced of Islam, yet Nabeel's curiosity toward Christianity was coming to a fever pitch. During a discussion, Nabeel began, "Ok, David, I can see that the New
Testament is accurate. I won't argue against that. However, I
do *not* see where Jesus Himself claimed to be God."

From there, the conversation turned toward historical
context and the Old Testament (The Hebrew Bible). He
wanted to avoid John 1 completely because there, John ob-
viously describes Jesus as God. To Nabeel, this meant very
little, as any writer could attribute anything they wanted to
Jesus. He wanted to find evidence that Christ described *Himself* in this manner. So Nabeel made his way to the Gospel
of Mark, specifically the 14th chapter. He read, "Jesus said,
'I AM. And you will see the Son of Man sitting at the right

hand of the Power, and coming with the clouds of heaven.'"

Here, in this passage, historical context and New Testament realities came together in an explosive revelation. Nabeel saw Jesus describing Himself as the *Son of Man*, a reference to the Messianic prophecy in Daniel. In this one verse, he saw the *I Am* statement from Exodus. He noticed the reference to God in Psalms 110, *coming with the clouds of heaven.*

It was clear that not only was Jesus declaring Himself to be God, but He did so in a manner that confirmed Old Testament prophecies that His Jewish audience would have instantly understood. He was not just walking around saying, "I am God, I am God," but utilizing the Jews' own Scriptures to unveil this truth.

Nabeel then understood that Jesus did claim to be God—it was irrefutable. But did He die upon a cross? In the Quran, the crucifixion is completely refuted: "That they said (in boast), 'We killed the Messiah Jesus the son of Mary, the Messenger of The God'; but they killed him not, nor crucified him..." (Surah An-Nisa 4:157). The problem he ran into was the reality that no matter how you look at it historically, every scholar and historian of any credibility all recognized that Jesus lived and that he was crucified by the Romans under Pontius Pilate. Even scholars who did not believe in Christ's divinity still acknowledged His very real life and death upon a cross.

All of this brought Nabeel to his third point of research:

the resurrection. It just so happened that a debate was being hosted locally near Old Dominion in Virginia between a Christian scholar who argued for the historical reality of the resurrection and an atheist who wanted to disprove the point. The Christian scholar took the audience through historical evidence, early documents, and recounted the behavior of the disciples following the resurrection and the testimony of the masses, who all concurred that they had seen Jesus alive after his verified death. Nabeel knew that he *could not* deny the resurrection. All of Nabeel's searching had brought him to the reality of an empty tomb.

Without a doubt, David had the upper hand in their multi-year debate. Nabeel came to terms with the fact that the Christian faith was far more compelling, though he was incredibly hesitant to embrace it. He described the hesitation as being "subconscious." He had grown up steeped in Muslim teachings that strictly warned against apostasy. All four of the Sunni schools of thought teach that apostates who embraced other gods outside of Allah should be killed. Three Shia schools of thought all confirmed the same thing. While this did not guarantee that his conversion would lead to being gunned down in the streets of America, it did mean that, according to Islam, he would be destined for hell. Worse yet, Nabeel felt he would be committing the ultimate act of betrayal toward his family. He would not just be leaving his Muslim religion, but his Muslim identity and heritage as an Islamic missionary.

While he may have been intellectually convinced by the faith, the cost slowed him down from moving forward. As a result, he prayed a risky prayer, saying, "God, tell me who You are. If You tell me to be a Christian, I will be one. If You give me a vision or dream and make it clear, I will follow You."

Over the course of three months, Nabeel had dreams and a vision which he would consider to be supernatural visitations from God—thoroughly convincing him of the merits of his research into Christianity. Sure, David made a good case for the faith, yet Nabeel's direct encounters sealed the deal. Prior to this journey, he had been happy with his Muslim faith and the Islamic community to which he belonged, but ultimately he became a follower of Jesus.

He later described his conversion as, "The most painful thing I ever did," losing most of his friendships and relationships with fellow Muslims, including connections with his own family. He was ultimately disowned, even by his own parents, and lived in a continual reminder of the price he was paying. Nabeel Qureshi went on to become an emerging Christian leader, teacher, and apologist—participating in public debates and lectures on the merits of Christianity versus Islam.

* * *

At this point in 2012, while in San Jose, I knew nothing of David, Nabeel Qureshi, or what a "Christian apologist" was, for that matter. I was completely ignorant of the aforementioned events, yet I would soon become aware. Through a mutual connection who knew I was searching for something more, I was told I should meet up with this mysterious "Nabeel" character. At the time, he was finishing his Master's Degree in theology at Biola and was yet to make a name for himself in Christian apologetics.

As I drove to Panera to meet with him, I knew I was going with plenty of ammunition. My six months of study had produced a number of questions, doubts, and concerns, and I had a list of apparent contradictions from the Bible that I was ready to bring up.

Despite having an Arabic name, I took note early in the meeting that he was Pakistani. In truth, people from Saudi Arabia generally do not have a high regard for people from Pakistan or India. To many in the Middle East, they are nothing more than drivers and blue-collar workers. Any preconceived notion I had of people from Pakistan was instantly dismantled as Nabeel began to speak. *Wow,* I thought, *this man is incredibly articulate.*

Before I had the chance to start in with my questions, he kept saying, "I need to share my story with you."

"I've heard these types of stories before," I replied. "You were a Muslim and then you became a Christian, and God changed you."

"No, no—it's more than that. I need to share my story

because I believe the story itself will answer many of your questions."

I nodded.

He started and continued, unpacking his background, experiences, and the highs and lows of his unique journey to faith. From debates with David to his time at Old Dominion, from the evidence of the resurrection to his family disowning him, Nabeel told all. And he was right—answers to many of my questions were found along the way as he shared.

As he finished sharing his testimony, I noticed something troubling—he had been through every stage of questioning, reading, criticizing, and searching that I had been through, and he was now a Christian. Internally, I began to question, *if I have been at every point he has, would I end up where he is now? Is my future Christianity?*

I hoped not.

I thanked him for telling his story. "We have a lot in common," I said. "I see why you wanted to share with me."

I explained that I had left Islam but had not landed anywhere else. He understood, and before long, I started in with my questions. I explained that I had been going to church and reading the Bible for hours and hours each week, and that I appreciated Jesus' teachings on love. I valued His treatment of women. Yet I had severe issues, "You claim that Jesus is pure with no sin, correct?"

"That's correct," he said.

"But he came from Mary, who had sin because she was of the seed of Adam. If he came from her, isn't He also polluted by sin?"

"Jesus was born from the Spirit of God," he explained. "Mary has little to do with it...she simply hosted Him."

Not a bad answer, I thought. But the questions were far from over.

"Islam taught me that Christians worship three Gods: the Father, Mary, and Jesus. Then I learned that Christians actually teach a different trinity: the Father, Son, and Holy Spirit. Islam teaches *one* God...Christianity teaches three, right?"

This was a question that I had posed to my Christian friends in the past. Some of them compared God to water, which can exist in different forms: frozen, steam, or liquid, but it's still water. These types of metaphors never seemed to satisfy, yet Nabeel gave an answer that did.

"We are made in God's image, Sahar. We have a body, a spirit, and a mind. You are a three-part being, just like God."

It was more than a metaphor—it was reality. I knew I was not three separate people but a single person with separate parts. If I am made in God's image, it would only make sense that God would be "triune" also.

During the talk, rather than being the typical "answer man" who knew every response, he said, "I want you to know, though, that Jesus wants to answer your questions more than I do. He loves you more than I could, or anyone could." He encouraged me to go to Jesus with questions. With my Islamic framework at play, something about going to Jesus had felt like a sort of idolatry in the past. Given that Jesus was a prophet in Islam, going to Him would be like a Christian going to Moses to ask questions.

"How about this," Nabeel said, "Go to the God who made you and talk to Him...ask Him about Jesus."

With this insight, I began to reconcile the Trinity even more and understand that God is indeed three-in-one. I started to accept the notion that Christians do not worship three Gods but *one* God in three persons. This sort of mystery can take time for anyone to sort out, especially someone from a hardline monotheistic background who had been raised to think that Christians were polytheists.

The meeting continued. At one point, he mentioned needing help with Arabic, so I gladly diverged from the discussion and assisted. He was taking an Arabic class so he could learn the language and read the Quran for himself, rather than relying on the English translation. We eventually paused for lunch, and the discussion continued afterward. In spite of my skepticism, my questions, my critiques, and my case, Nabeel was offering answers that satisfied my inquiry on a level that I had not experienced prior. After a full seven-hour meeting, I closed with a final line of questioning that had to do with what I considered to be a *weakness* on God's part.

"Nabeel, your God is weak. Why would He have a Son?

Then put Himself in the womb of a human like me? How can a majestic and powerful God become a weak little baby? And then volunteer to be killed? That's humiliating."

I was so adamant on the subject that I avoided reading about the crucifixion in my Bible time. In fact, outside the bedroom window of my apartment, there was a church on a hill with a large cross visible from my bed. At night, when it was time to sleep, I would turn away from the window, so as not to face the cross.

Nabeel tackled my hesitancy toward the cross head-on, and his response was twofold. First, he provided some backdrop on the remission of sins in the Hebrew world and the built-in need for a blood sacrifice. He then added a crucial piece, "Jesus died because of love."

"I don't see love, I see weakness," I rebutted, "and I don't want to follow a weak God."

"It's not weakness. It's love. Let me give you an example. Imagine you're dressed up to go to an important event. You're majestic, clean, and robed in the best. But then you see your child has fallen into a hole and is stuck. Would you jump in and help, or would you ignore your child?"

"I would go in myself," I said.

"Is that weakness on your part, to muddy your dress and leave your proper place to help your child?"

"No. It would not be weakness. It would be love," I had to admit.

Suddenly, the dots connected, and I could see that this

act of crucifixion was not weakness but the strongest act of love. God left His prestige and majesty to muddy Himself in our world, to demonstrate His love and grace toward us. I couldn't wiggle out of this reality: it *was* love. It *is* love. It *will always* be love.

The analogy opened my eyes to see the truth in the gospel that I had been blind to for so long. Nabeel told me that God is love, peace, and truth. He explained that because of sin, we are separated from God and added, "If you just put your faith in Jesus, you will have a relationship with the Father forever. Just accept what Jesus did for you."

"It seems so simple," I said.

"Simple does not mean *easy*," he assured me. "The Christian life is not easy. It's a life of holiness, and it's a hard path, but God is with you every step. Being a Muslim rule-follower at times is easier than walking with a holy God. There is no personal relationship required in Islam, just religious boxes to check. Holiness in the Bible is different than holiness in Islam because Christianity deals with the internal life."

I left the meeting feeling like my "internal life" was actively being upended. I went home and was puzzled by this new sense of clarity. Nabeel had answered everything effortlessly. My objections were squashed. I felt that I had just spent the day in the presence of authentic spirituality. Just being around him caused some sense of heaven to rub off on me. Seven hours is a long time to meet with a man who knew and loved Jesus, and I felt like every step I took was on holy ground in some sense.

After entering my apartment, I again opened the Bible to find this love that Nabeel spoke of. In Saudi, our King always travels with someone of the same blood type who can give the King an organ or transfusion if an emergency happens—sacrificially giving his life for the sake of the King. In Islam, the highest calling is to be a martyr in Jihad for God's sake. Here, in the Christian Scriptures, I found a reversal—God was a King who made the sacrifice and died for His people.

I opened the New Testament to 1 John and read the letter. It was *all* love. I dared to pray to Jesus Christ for the very first time, "Jesus, if you are God and this book is true, show me and I will follow You."

Suddenly, in an instant, I felt the presence of God. How can I describe such an event? I felt *completely* and *totally* seen and known by God in the most real way imaginable. He knew that I was searching. It was so real, I felt as though Jesus were standing directly behind me. In a fit of emotion, I was crying and laughing, laughing and crying. In the most tangible way possible, I felt joy in finding Jesus as well as sorrow for the wasted years toiling in Islam. I arrived at 1 John 4 and read, "There is no fear in love. But perfect love drives out fear, because fear has to do with punishment. The one who fears is not made perfect in love."

Until then, I had always been afraid of death, afraid of

God, and even afraid of heaven itself. Yet here I was, basking in perfect love and sensing all fear being taken away for the first time in my life. In that moment, I gave Jesus my entire life, my present, my past, my dreams, my relationships, my possessions, my studies, my highs, my lows, my good, my bad, my plans, my hopes, and my future. It was all *His.*

I went to my bedroom and lay down, feeling happily loved by God. I then felt something negative, demonic even, and looked to the right. There on my small bookshelf, I took note of the stack of Qurans I had. A voice within me spoke, "I don't want those in your bedroom." I took all of my Qurans and threw them in the trash, except one. The one I kept, I placed in the bathroom. Islam teaches that bathrooms are unclean and God's presence is not there anyway. So I placed the one keepsake Quran in the bathroom. I had a lot to learn.

And just like that, I was 27 years old and a newborn Christian.

I lay down in my bed and gazed out the window at the hilly city. There was the church, which I had seen so often. In their front yard was the cross, shining with a blazing light, elevated high. It was the only thing I could see from my window. That night, the cross meant something different. It was not a myth or a weakness. It meant *love,* and nothing hinders God's love. There in the bed, on that fateful night, I did what I had never done: I turned toward the cross, closed my eyes, and slept.

CHAPTER NINE

Me Again

Alive, Passionate, and Fired Up

"There is no other salvation except that which begins and ends with grace."

—CHARLES SPURGEON

The following morning, I awoke to the realization that everything was now different. I had spent seven months searching after leaving Islam, and what I found at the end of my search was the end of myself. Decades of indoctrination had taught me that if I properly purified myself, I could then cautiously approach a holy God who was likely in a bad mood anyway—but at least this God might tolerate me if I was sure to take every step perfectly. Yet now my doctrine had finally been flipped, and I could see that there was nothing I could do to save myself. Jesus Himself purified us by extending salvation to mankind when we were without hope. Purification was not needed *before* prayer, but was found *within* the prayer as I came to God. Where Islam had taught that we must clean ourselves before coming to God, Christianity taught that God Himself *is* the glorious shower, cleaning us with His presence and grace.

I got out of bed, fully aware of the newfound presence of God in my life, and that awareness has never left. I ate and got dressed as usual and went for a walk, only to find that everything appeared different. Trees were more beautiful, and the sky glowed with a novel brilliance. Nature itself had not changed overnight, of course, but my *perception* of everything had changed, knowing that I was the beloved daughter of the One who created it all.

I was connected to God, and a new *life* was pulsing through me that I had never known. This life was not the fact that breath was in my lungs or the fact that my heart was beating. This *life* was from above and in an instant had changed my state from merely existing to truly living. I bubbled with joy, fervor for life, and a love I had never known. It became clear that I could not give what I did not have, and now that I had received the greatest love imaginable, I felt poised to share that love as well. A tenderness grew within me for others. I sensed a certain invincibility in my spirit. I was no longer afraid of God, of death, and of man, and that fear had been replaced with a peaceful security that made my walk lighter, my voice more confident, and my smile more genuine.

I loved what I was experiencing and did not want anyone to touch it or take it away. I've been a private person my whole life—in fact, we have a saying in Arabic that I always took to heart, "داري على شمعتك تقيد" which translates, "Protect your candle so it won't go out." As a result, I grew to not like the spotlight or thrive on admiration and recognition. To people with this upbringing, being noticed feels less like a compliment and more like an irritation that disrupts a carefully crafted internal life. It feels like the moment I step into the spotlight, I am a public product who loses ownership over my own identity. So, from before my conversion to after, I have always valued autonomy and fiercely protected the life I've carved on my terms.

As a result, I spoke of my conversion to no one in those first few days. I felt that in my silence, I could savor what I was feeling and make it last longer. By refusing to reveal my newfound faith, it seemed that I could protect the experience from strife, argument, and division. *How would my family react? What does this mean for my Muslim friends?*

My mother already pushed back at my skepticism toward Islam; how much more would she rage now that I had come to Christianity? Rather than face these questions, I lived in my satisfaction with Jesus alone for those first honeymoon days. The only thing that seemed to interrupt this blissful state of being were the moments of grief I would feel for the years I spent outside of this reality and the sorrow I would feel for those who were still there. In fact, my heart overflowed with a new love for people, which was intense and palpable.

Eventually, I began sharing the truth of who Jesus is with others. Suddenly, the things that my Christian friends did that I had always felt were crazy, I was now doing regularly. Whether it was sharing my testimony with a stranger or praying for someone in a restaurant, I dove headfirst into this lifestyle. I had gone from snickering at the crazy, passionate Christians to becoming one myself. Everywhere I looked, I questioned whether or not the people around me knew Jesus and felt I had a duty to make sure.

Around the time I got saved, it was Ramadan, a holy month in Islam. I did not fast, which my mom was fully aware of. To her chagrin, I had disregarded Islamic customs for some time; however, because of my initial silence, she was not aware of my newfound faith in Jesus. During a routine Skype call, she encouraged me, "Go back to the right path, Sahar. You need to fast."

I shrugged off the encouragement, and she brought it up again, "You're not fasting, huh?"

I told her I was *not,* but did not tell her why.

"Your face has changed," she said. "You have light in your face. Where are you sitting?"

I told her I was sitting in the same spot as I always had during our calls.

"No," she insisted, "something is different—there is a light upon you."

In an instant, a connection was made in my mind between what she had just noticed and what I had been reading in Scripture. "Mom," I said. "I'm reading the Bible, and Jesus says we are the light of the world."

There was a pause, and she looked at me carefully, then asked a question that she likely did not want to hear the answer to: "Are you a Christian now, Sahar?"

I hesitated. "Yes, I am." I couldn't help it, but while saying this, I had a *big* smile across my face. It was not spiteful, but full of uncontainable joy.

Click.

She hung up.

I could have been crushed, broken, and in despair over the rejection. But in truth, nothing could steal the joy I was feeling in Jesus, not even her hanging up on me. My gladness remained, even in the weeks to come, which were fraught with tension and personal attacks. My time in the Scriptures would be interrupted with a text from my mother, saying something like, "You're out of your mind, what are you thinking?" or "I wish I had never birthed you." Messages would flood in, filled with anger, disappointment, and even hatred. I had known my mother to be a harsh figure, but this was an entirely different level of vitriol. I truly understood that I no longer belonged in this world, but that I belonged to another Kingdom! I realized that those trapped in Islam have no Father, no identity, and no inheritance.

She expressed that she had failed in her duties as a parent. Knowing how devout I was to the Christian faith, she feared the worst: my siblings turning away from Islam as well. Sometimes I would reply as amicably as possible; other times, my responses only heightened the strain between us. On one occasion, I had shared with her my doubts about certain teachings in the Quran, questioning its interpretations. This only incited further anger in her. She began urging my siblings to cut off communication with me, which would act as both a punishment to me and a protection to them.

My siblings believed it was just a temporary phase and that I would eventually snap out of it.

"No," I would say, "I have encountered God."

My insistence was not well received by them. They found it improbable that I had "met God," to say the least. After all, in the Islamic worldview, meeting God was an experience reserved for the prophets of old, not someone like me, a woman in the 21st century. Who was I to think I had become acquainted with the Creator of the universe?

As I forged ahead in daily prayer, Bible reading, and worship, I found that my personality was changing. Boldness began to supplant the shy, backward tendencies that I had lived with for so long. The little girl who sat confidently in her daddy's lap was now returning, walking with boldness in her Heavenly Father's love.

For the first time in my life, I began to reconcile with my childhood. As I looked back, I saw my father. I remembered the unique prayers, the photo of Jesus, and the personal, friend-like devotion he maintained with God. It was clear that my father had a secret, and that secret was a true, personal devotion to the Christian faith. His kindness and goodness were evident to all who knew him. Bear in mind, this good nature came from a man who had been completely abandoned and set up for failure.

For him to be the softhearted person that he was, he had to be drawing on a source that was greater than his childhood. This source had to be greater than the dysfunction he knew all too well. When, as a child, I would behold that photo of Jesus that he had placed in our room, I was looking at my dad's very source of strength, hope, love, and kindness. Here I was, at the age of 28, and my father's source had become my own. This Jesus, whom he secretly followed and studied, had responded to my search. While I thought I was the one pursuing and searching, I came to discover that He was the one pursuing and searching for me all along. I was rapidly changing and growing, unlearning lies and soaking up truth. I began to not only know God, but for the first time, to know myself.

The tears that had been frozen after my dad's death began to thaw when I came to Christ, being released from their long-held frost. I had spent most of my life ignoring my feelings and suppressing any and all emotions. My upbringing did not afford many spaces for emotional vulnerability; feelings were to be mastered, not obeyed. Yet here I was, letting my tears have their due course. God was allowing me to *feel* again.

For a year after my conversion, I found that tears came easily to my eyes. My heart swelled with tenderness, and the emotions that I had repressed for so long were coming back and manifesting. With a Bible open in front of me and my eyes wet with tears, I might have looked wounded and broken on the outside, but inside I was being deeply and completely *healed*.

In those quiet places of prayer, I found God's presence filling and healing the chasms of old wounds in my heart. The words of the Bible, so different from the Quran I grew up reciting, spoke of healing and forgiveness, of seas parting and bread multiplying, and most importantly, of a Savior's love that bears all things, believes all things, hopes all things, and endures all things.

I let myself weep over verses that promised me peace, a peace that whispered through the ancient text and into the depths of my being. Each teardrop told a story of release, of chains breaking, of God showing up. In the sacred place of prayer, I found that my prayers became conversations, filled with the raw, unpolished thoughts of a heart that was learning to speak freely. The curiosity that I had as a little girl was now coming back in full force. The endless questions I had for my dad, which ceased in my adolescence, had returned, and I found that God was able to handle my wide-ranging inquiries.

When Jesus became my Lord, I became *me again*. I was no longer hiding or running from God, myself, or others, but living in the wonderful security that Jesus purchased for me. I began to see that the old version of me was not just in the past but was dead. Just a couple of days after my salvation, I had an experience that would forever imprint this truth into my mind. During a conversation with Jesus, I experienced what can only be described as an *open vision*. I was fully conscious, awake, and my eyes were open, yet I saw a very clear picture of a grave, and I knew at once that it was mine.

"Are you telling me I'll be killed, God?"

I opened the Scriptures and read a passage from Paul which said, "to live is Christ, and to die is gain" (Philippians 1:21). I instantly knew God was saying I had been crucified with Christ and was dead to the flesh but alive unto Him. I realized that my past, with its fears and constraints, no longer defined who I was or who I could be. In Christ, I had found a new identity, one that transcended the boundaries of culture and the expectations that had once shackled me. No longer bound by the old self, I was free to live with a heart fully committed to the path God had laid before me. I learned what it meant to be born again. Having the Spirit of God reside in me opened heaven in my life, and now I can see the unseen. Only He can define me and my purposes.

The pairing of these visual experiences and the Scriptures I was reading began to affirm and embolden my faith.

A few weeks before I had gotten saved, the pastor's mom at the Arabic Christian Church in San Jose approached me and said, "Sahar, you are clearly seeking truth. Jesus is faithful. When you know Him, be faithful to Him."

Her words echo within me to this day. May the sum total of my experiences in God result in a steadfast faithfulness to Him as He has been faithful to me. The first year of my salvation felt like living ten years in one. I spent the overwhelming majority of my time in the Bible, seeking God, worshiping, and studying in solitude. Beyond that, I spent much time answering the questions of my Muslim friends as to why I left Islam.

When I finally broke my silence, I recall telling them, "I would rather tell you about my Christianity and you leave me than withhold this from you and remain your friend." I never attacked Islam, I was not aggressive, but I did advocate for truth, and this was hard for many of them to hear. I was intense, no doubt, and wound up losing all of my friends except one—a fellow Saudi named Hussien who is as close as a brother. To this day, he remains curious toward the faith and kind in our dealings.

Quickly, I discovered that I was not alone in my conversion. God swept through my family with a mighty move of the Spirit and began bringing more of my family to Himself. Within weeks of my salvation, several relatives of mine came to Christianity as well. Dreams and visions of Jesus and Christian concepts began blossoming in the lives of those near me. On multiple occasions, I had family come to visit me, and I could sense they came on a mission to help me deconstruct my Christian faith and return to Islam. With each meeting, they left changed and refreshed, and my faith in Jesus was bolstered all the more.

From grace to mercy, from repentance to spiritual gifts, I was being schooled in the rich teachings of the New Covenant. Both from trusted voices and from my own private studies, I was learning more in the faith in a short burst than I had ever learned at the university. One of the teachers at the English church also began to disciple me. I would tell her about the dreams and visions I was having, and she would validate the voice of God in them and encourage me to write down what was happening.

I recall her teaching me much about forgiveness and the importance of releasing those who have wronged us. The Christian faith teaches that love does not keep track of wrongdoings, whereas Islam has a built-in culture of keeping grudges. I saw the contrast between the obligatory prayer of Islam and the free-flowing, relational prayer of Christianity. The security I sensed in my salvation was internal and unshaking—a far cry from the insecurity and fear I felt toward salvation in my youth. I noticed compassion toward leaders in the church, toward those outside of the faith, and a true care for their souls. Unlike my upbringing, those of other faiths—or no faith at all—were not referred to as infidels and cast-offs.

While I noticed the differences between Islam and Christianity, I should note that my conversion was not a reactionary rebellion against Islam. Remember, I did not go from Islam to Christianity; I went from Islam to nothing, then later to Christianity. My growth process was not occupied by a constant comparison of the Muslim world and the Christian one. I was not drawn to the differences between my new faith and my old one; I was drawn to Jesus Christ.

For me, the New Testament was easy reading in my first year of Christianity. I spent most of my time studying the life of Jesus and placing 100% of my focus on Him. I would sit and read the Bible and ask Jesus questions. I worked through the gospels, the epistles, and would re-read them many times through. Prior to being saved, I had read the Bible, but it was usually a dry experience as I came with a critical eye, looking to find fault and contradiction. Now, though, the Scriptures were alive, vibrant, and pulsing with life. I now had the Spirit in me and could enjoy the Bible the way it was meant to be enjoyed.

I did wrestle with the Old Testament (The Hebrew Bible) quite a lot in those early days. Many of the stories, customs, and ideas seemed foreign, contrary to Christianity, and difficult to grasp. By studying and listening, I realized that the Old Testament (The Hebrew Bible) must be understood with a New Testament lens. In fact, the New Testament is full of cross-references and quotations from the

Old. I discovered the benefit of listening to Messianic Jews as they gave new light to the Old Testament (The Hebrew Bible) that a modern Gentile could not.

In studying Jewish customs, I came to have a better appreciation for the New Testament and Old alike. For instance, I struggled for some time to understand the words of Jesus when He said, "But concerning that day and hour no one knows, not even the angels of heaven, nor the Son, but the Father only" (Matthew 24:36). It seemed that Jesus was lowering Himself as less than God and forfeiting His all-knowing nature. I could not find a satisfactory answer among standard American preachers, and eventually happened upon a little booklet that spoke of marriage in the ancient Jewish culture. To my surprise, the answer I needed was found in it.

In the Jewish custom, the father sets the day of the wedding. The bride would get ready every night for her husband, knowing marriage could happen on any day. Once she was prepared, the groom would arrive, and they would inform her, "He is here."

In essence, the groom is waiting on the dad, and the bride is waiting on the groom. When they come together in marriage, they meet in the air as they are lifted up on the shoulders of friends and family—a tradition that still happens in Jewish culture. When the Bible describes us meeting Jesus in the air (see 1 Thessalonians 4:17), it is depicting a *wedding*. Jesus was giving us a glimpse of extraordinary bridal love. I could sense Jesus asking me, "Are you ready for me *daily*?"

When Jesus describes the Father knowing the hour, He is not making a statement about His lack of omnipotence or lowering Himself below God. He is simply describing a wedding which those who heard Him at the time would have fully understood.

For myself and many others, we would never know these truths without the help of Jewish resources. The majority of the Bible was written from a Jewish perspective, and as I grew in the faith, I realized it was critical to adopt this hermeneutic[16] in my studies. In the same way that I was critical and questioning of my faith in Islam, I was critical of certain Christian preachers and ideas. I guarded myself, making sure I only took in sermons, books, and resources that jived with Scripture and reflected the character of God. I studied with fervor and passion, not just to gain head knowledge but to better grasp this infinite God who had so captured my heart.

Within that first year of being saved, I wanted to be baptized but had made up my mind to read the entire Bible before doing so, determined to know my faith as well as possible before making a public confession. While in Virginia visiting friends, I attended an Arabic church that was led by a pastor whom I had deep respect for. I knew I wanted him

---

16. A hermeneutic is the method we use for interpreting the Bible.

to baptize me.

He agreed, of course, and the baptism took place at the home of a Lebanese woman, a godly and kind widow who graciously opened her home to me. Her backyard provided an intimate setting, with only a few close friends in attendance. The sacrament of baptism appealed to me as it was not a performance-based constant washing like dua prayers. In fact, it was not a cleansing but a symbol of the *internal* cleansing that Jesus had brought into my life. With a few friends and the glory of God present, right there in the shallow water of an inflatable swimming pool, I was immersed and brought up into a new life.

* * *

Some time after coming to faith, I was visiting friends at Biola University. The school sits between Los Angeles and Anaheim in Southern California. It has been a Christian education center for over a hundred years, with several notable alumni. At the time, Nabeel was teaching there and working on his book *Seeking Allah, Finding Jesus,* which would come out and make waves as a New York Times Bestseller.

We had not spoken since our day-long meeting. I found him on campus and told him, "Nabeel, I'm following Jesus now!"

He was surprised and elated, "Come here, come here," he said. "I'm teaching a class right now. Can you come in and share with the students?"

I walked in and he said to the class, "I don't remember what I told her during our meeting, but I'm just now finding out she has come to Christianity from Islam. This wasn't planned, but Sahar is going to share her story with you all."

This public speaking engagement was so sudden that I did not have time to be nervous. I dove into my story and related the journey with those in the room, detailing the meeting with Nabeel, the reality of God's presence, and how everything had changed since. From the corner of my eye, I noticed tears in Nabeel's eyes as he wept while I shared. At the end of the class, he said to me, "All I knew about you when we met was that you were a Saudi Muslim with questions." He then added, "You are not an ordinary follower of Jesus. You have greatness, you have a high calling, Sahar."

After meeting at Biola, he and I stayed in touch. It's not an exaggeration to say he had a true hand in discipling me. I recall him answering my questions, I would listen to his messages, and I even adopted some of the language he used in his debates. If a lifelong Christian became an apologist who debated with Muslims, it would feel less compelling than a lifelong Muslim like Nabeel. He was a voice for so many who needed to see the combination of intellectual fervor, theological accuracy, and loving passion for the faith. To me, Nabeel was not just a loving and caring brother in the family of God. He was an example of suffering, perseverance, and trust and faith in God.

The week before he passed away, the Holy Spirit had me reading Hebrews 11 and 12 constantly—daily, even. I remember wondering why God had me read these two chapters nonstop! After Nabeel's passing, I read them again, and I understood that we are high priests in the Kingdom of God, that we are like Melchizedek, and Jesus is the forerunner on our behalf (see Hebrews 6:19-20). Melchizedek had no earthly mother or father. His source was God. I sensed that, like Melchizedek, I was fully adopted by God, led by the Spirit, and not defined by the flesh. Another verse that stood out to me was, "The world is not worthy of them" (see Hebrew 11:38). I believe that like my dad, Nabeel did not see the things promised by God, just like their brothers and sisters in the faith before them—they are in the cloud of witnesses, cheering us on, praying, and interceding for us as Hebrews 11 describes.

I studied the Scriptures and found passages like, "Before I formed you in the womb I knew you, and before you were born I consecrated you; I appointed you a prophet to the nations" (Jeremiah 1:5). I noted Scriptures that stated, "And he made from one man every nation of mankind to live on all the face of the earth, having determined allotted periods and the boundaries of their dwelling place, that they should seek God, and perhaps feel their way toward him and find him. Yet he is actually not far from each one of us" (Acts 17:26-27).

I thought: *God chose my gender, my family, my gifts,*

strengths, weaknesses, and where I would be born. I meditated on the Scripture that said, "For we are his workmanship, created in Christ Jesus for good works, which God prepared beforehand, that we should walk in them" (Ephesians 2:10).

So I prayed, "What were You thinking when You made me, Lord? What did You have in mind for me?" I had the sense that my life would be more than an American degree or a career in business management at a firm in California. I just didn't know exactly how things would take shape. The clues came together in bits and pieces. Shortly after my salvation in 2012, I asked Jesus what He saw in me and who He made me to be. In response, He showed me a beautiful lily growing by a body of water.

"You need to be connected to Me so this flower can grow and stay healthy." I watched as the flower grew and grew and became big. The petals fell off, and women ran to grab them. The more the women came to grab the petals, the more the flower grew, and additional petals were produced. These soft petals brought healing to those who took them. Slowly, my purpose was being revealed to me. I knew that I would have a ministry of healing—healing of the heart, soul, and the interior life. This ministry would emphasize the restoration of honor and nobility, would give voice to the voiceless, and would create hope where none existed.

Of course, it's easy to have a ministry vision. It's something else entirely to create blueprints and discover what it actually looks like to carry out that ministry. This particular vision was born from the Spirit of God Himself, marked by passion and power beyond my understanding. Early on, opportunities to speak and share my testimony began opening up, and I leapt at the chance to do so, feeling both a sense of duty and excitement.

Traveling around my area of northern California, I was welcomed into a variety of churches, ministries, and small gatherings from little chapels to larger auditoriums in bustling cities. Each invitation brought a unique congregation eager to hear about my journey from Saudi Arabia to Christianity in America. As I stood at the pulpit before rows of curious and compassionate faces, I recounted my story of discovery, struggle, and ultimately, transformation through Jesus. This experience not only deepened my own faith but also connected me with diverse communities of Christians.

On one occasion, a lady approached and said, "When I heard you speaking, I felt the Lord say that you are going to serve Him in ministry."

"Yeah, He told me that too...but not yet. I'm not ready."

At that point in time, I was still working standard jobs that related to my degree and area of focus. Through a woman in the company, I got connected to a Christian in Corona who started a business and wanted someone to work with him in IT and sales. He was an Arab believer with a Christian background, and from his family, I felt he had a good reputation. I was intrigued and told him, "I want a job that's flexible so I can serve God in ministry but also have an income."

"Of course we support that," he said. "We will be flexible. If you need a break to go speak or do ministry, we will flex your hours accordingly."

I had already moved across the world and then across America multiple times, so a six-hour shift south to Corona felt reasonable. With the promise of a job, ministry prospects, *and* an apartment that would be paid for by the company, I left the Bay Area for good.

CHAPTER TEN

Unveiling Beauty

Launched

"Who you know really impacts what you know."
—Sally Krawcheck

Unfortunately, the job did not pan out. The promises made were not promises kept, and the company struggled. The pay was far less than originally told, and the job itself felt like a secretary/errand runner position rather than anything IT-related. While the main owner was a Christian, others in leadership were Muslim, and they fought often—running hot and cold, leaving the small staff of employees nervous about our place on the team. The screaming wasn't pleasant to hear, and could actually be defined as emotional abuse. There seemed to be an attitude from the top down that I should be happy that I had a job at all and that the misrepresentation should just be ignored.

After two months, I drove to work one day and prayed,

"God, what is this? I feel like a slave." At that moment, I sensed that I was released to move on. Even then, I went back to my dad's loving standard from childhood and refused to be treated less than I was worth. I gave my resignation, and within a year, the company closed.

Lesson learned: Don't be tricked by a Christian label. Just because someone claims a Christian title does not mean they will be following through with Christian action. I had committed to an apartment, a job, and a move based on the promise of man rather than discerning the individual's character. Nevertheless, God was in on it, as He had plans for me in that region. He used the situation to bring me to the place He wanted me for the time being.

My dear friend Elias, from Palestine, had moved to the area a few years prior. I knew him from Chico, and we remained good friends over time—he felt like a brother. He wore a big cross necklace and had long hair to his shoulders. He spoke Arabic and had explained the gospel to me in the past, which had always fallen on deaf ears. Now, though, our friendship was strengthened even more by our common faith in Christ.

With a failed job and no place to stay, I asked Elias if he had any ideas. He told me he knew of a family with a big house in the area that invited people to stay with them, sometimes for extended periods. They were all Christians living together communally, studying the Bible, and having meals together. This alone appealed to me, as I had not been able to find the communal aspect of Saudi culture here in the States. I quickly reached out and explained my situation.

"Come stay with us," I heard on the other end, "we have a room for you."

With suitcases clutched tightly in hand, I arrived at the door and took in the sprawling home, which felt like a welcoming embrace from the start. Drew and Nancy, who owned the place, had a remarkable testimony in their own right. They had both been left in previous marriages, and after finding each other, they discovered God's purpose for their union. They were supportive of one another, and their love for each other—and for each of their guests—was palpable. They radiated warmth and kindness. I was ushered to my room, shown around, and extended an invitation to eat dinner with the rest of the people.

As I made myself comfortable, I looked around the house and observed that the property almost felt like a museum as it was packed full of beautiful artwork. In fact, they hosted an art club once a month with musicians, jewelry makers, and painters. Nancy was an artist herself, and Drew taught script writing at a nearby school.

Our mornings began with group devotions and prayers, setting the tone for the day. Evenings were marked by shared dinner duties, with each resident taking turns to prepare meals—except on Fridays, which were reserved for personal time. Drew and Nancy led with curiosity, always kindly asking about my background, culture, customs, norms, and my family. In fact, when my mother and brother visited a year later, they too were given rooms and embraced with great hospitality, being treated as if they were long-standing members of the household.

We studied books and discussed what we read. I was growing in my understanding of God *and* in my understanding of myself. *The Road Back to You* had a big impact on me. The book takes the results of the Enneagram personality test and links them back to Scripture and Christianity. I began to learn about myself and understand my past, my motivations, and why I was the way I was. Pascal, a Christian writer and inventor, wrote, "One must know oneself... there is nothing better." I had grown up in a system that stifled self-reflection. Because I did not know *myself*, I did not know how I related to others. I found that knowing myself improved my relationships, my ministry efforts, and my life as a whole.

During my 18 months in the house, I gathered more than just information from books or deeper insight in the Bible—I learned the value of *community*. This time reinforced the fact that I was not just part of a religion, but I was woven into the fabric of a vibrant global community of believers who cared for one another.

As my vision expanded, the ministry picked up pace. Drew and Nancy generously allowed me to use their home for ministry and encouraged the gifts God put within me.

Each ministry has its own unique angle, and during this season, I began to find mine. Some are called to do street outreach in New York. Others are called to medical missions in Mozambique. Anyone who has sensed the call of God to ministry knows that there is time spent seeking the Lord to discern *who* you are called to be, *what* you are called to do, and *where* you are called to carry it out.

Shortly after getting saved and while still in Colorado, I had heard about a ministry called *Fashion Meets Faith,* where the intersection of style and Christianity was explored through events and training. It sounded right up my alley, and I wanted to hear more. I approached Sherri, the image consultant who ran the ministry, and said, "I love fashion. And Jesus. I want to be involved in a fashion ministry like this."

"That's amazing," she replied. "We need someone who speaks Spanish on board with us. I'll pay for you to come to my training."

I then explained that I was not Mexican, but Arab, and a former Muslim.

"Oh, I love Muslims. Same deal—I'll pay for your training. Come on out!"

The training was a five-day process. I was given a book and swatches and trained in how to identify a person's best colors. I won't bog down the book here with a long chapter on color theory in fashion, but basically, depending on things like skin tone, hair shade, eye color, and so forth, each person has a color palette that is most flattering that they should build their wardrobe around. Most women know that the right dress in the wrong color is the wrong dress.

Sherri taught that Christian women should represent themselves and God properly. We should aim to have not only the right beliefs and the right thinking but also the right presentation. If God is a God of excellence and splendor, why should we be a sloppy people—given that we are to represent Him to the world? In the Old Testament (The Hebrew Bible), Esther went through a year-long beautification process, which positioned her to be seen properly and to fulfill the plan of God for her life.

The combination of fashion, beauty, and creating atmospheres for prayer, and sharing the truths of God struck me as novel and brilliant. During that season, I found myself in need of work—work that offered both flexibility and financial stability. I would typically search for something in my area of focus—IT management—but given these new developments, I began to think outside the box.

Cabi, a company selling high-quality, expensive clothes, caught my attention. They sold clothing not through traditional stores but through personal sales representatives. Given my recent entry into the world of fashion and image consulting, I was hopeful to be part of Cabi's team. I sent them an email letting them know my interest.

The process was simple: you purchased clothes, hosted parties for women to try them on, and took their orders. It was a business model that promised both social engagement, opportunities to share the gospel, and independence. I would make good money and enjoy the freedom of scheduling parties at my convenience, totally avoiding the nine-to-five routine.

Joanne, a Cabi rep for the entire region, responded to my email with warmth. "Would love to meet you in person," she wrote. At the time, my email had a Scripture in the signature, "There is no fear in love, but perfect love casts out fear" (I John 4:18).

Very quickly, I received a reply in which she gave me her number and urged me to call her immediately. On the phone, she asked, "I see the Scripture. Are you a Christian?" I replied that I was indeed, and then shared some of my story with her. I discovered that Joanne had previously lived in Dubai, and that she and her husband harbored a shared mission: to spread the gospel in the UAE. Our first meeting was serendipitous, filled with conversations about God, the Middle East, and scarcely a word about the Cabi business that brought us together in the first place. From that moment, our partnership blossomed into a ministry.

I, with my connections to Middle Eastern women, and Joanne, with her ties to American women, created a unique fellowship where we utilized each other's networks and strategized best practices for the ministry. We visited homes, shared our faith, engaged in deep conversations, and conducted our Cabi business along the way. These clothing parties became a sanctuary for ministry, where commerce and compassion came together.

When God places a ministry calling upon an individual, He always follows up by providing people and provision. We are not supposed to do this alone, and at every step of my journey and my entry into ministry, God has supplied *people* to play key roles. Doors open when God knows we are willing to walk through.

Prophetic activity has marked so much of my relationship with Jesus. Even early after getting saved, when I had little understanding of spiritual gifts, I found myself in the throes of intense dreams and visions from the Lord. In this season, as ministry was ramping up, I felt I was on the precipice of launching my own organization. Sure enough, God spoke to me with a powerful dream.

In it, I was walking in an airport. I was aware that Jesus was walking behind me and telling me exactly where to go. "Turn left, turn right," and I would do so accordingly. Faces from all over the world were there. Eventually, He directed me to turn right and enter an airplane. The passengers were all women and were all covered head-to-toe in the Saudi way. Jesus allowed me to have glimpses of their souls. I was deeply sad for them.

"Where are you going?" I asked the passengers.

"We don't know," one responded.

"Who's your pilot?" I followed up.

"We don't know."

From behind me, I heard the voice of Jesus saying, "They're waiting for you. The time is now." Suddenly, the scene changed, and I was cooking frantically for this group, and they were insatiably hungry. I would serve food, and they would have it consumed before I could finish cooking the next dish.

I woke up knowing a few things. First, my people, women in Saudi and the Middle East, are without direction. These women have no pilot and no path. Second, I knew they were starving for purpose, fulfillment, and the truths of the gospel, and I would be the one to serve them. The time to launch was not the day before or a month later, but then and there.

What is the name of this ministry? I wondered.

Each day, as I pondered the countless women, both near and far, who remained unaware of their God-given beauty, my vision for ministry crystallized. Women throughout the Middle East were not only physically veiled from the public but spiritually veiled as well. A psalm began to echo in my heart day after day: "Hear, O daughter, and consider, and incline your ear: forget your people and your father's house, and the king will desire your beauty. Since he is your lord, bow to him" (Psalm 45:10-11). I knew then, the Lord was calling me to something big—something that would require me to leave my things behind and follow after Him—fully enthroning Him as the King of my life.

The truth is, my family was a big hindrance to my calling early on. I feared disappointing my family back home—my mom especially—but I knew the calling of God upon my life was bigger than my fear. Jesus said, "No one who puts his hand to the plow and looks back is fit for the kingdom of God" (Luke 9:62).

At one point during Jesus' ministry, someone told him, "Your mother and brothers are standing outside, wanting to speak to you." He replied, "'Who is my mother, and who are my brothers?' Pointing to his disciples, he said, 'Here are my mother and my brothers. For 'whoever does the will of my Father in heaven is my brother and sister and mother'" (Matthew 12:47-50).

With these truths cemented in my being, I moved ahead. My heart ached as I thought of the masses of women living lives cloaked in obscurity, unaware of their inherent worth, beauty, and value. It was then, after training under Sherri and doing ministry with Joanne, that God showed me the name of my ministry. The name itself would serve a double purpose, emphasizing the beauty of Jesus that's hidden from Muslim women and calling to mind the literal veil that covers the beauty of those same women. Thus, was born: *Unveiling Beauty*.

* * *

Joanne knew that God was orchestrating something profound in my life, and I was open with her about my ministry goals. She introduced me to Shirin Taber, a believer from a Muslim home with an Iranian father and American mother. Shirin's ministry was dedicated to aiding believers in their new journeys, and she focused her efforts on the Middle East and North Africa, and eventually Iran and Pakistan.

Upon our meeting, Shirin asked many, many questions about my vision. I told her I had a name, a target group of women whom I would lead and teach about Jesus, but little else. I didn't know the first thing about formalizing and launching an organization. She then connected me to the Global Service Association (GSA), an organization designed to support new ministries. GSA's framework allowed new organizations to set up accounts, raise funds, and exist under their umbrella. If necessary, these organizations could then launch into their own independent 501(c)(3) entities. Rich, the founder of the ministry, became a pivotal figure in that season. In fact, he and Joanne are on my board to this day.

Fundraising became my immediate challenge. The task was daunting, as Middle Easterners are more quiet about their money. While generosity abounds within our community, the act of soliciting funds felt foreign and uncomfortable. I knew pastors who juggled full-time jobs with their pastoral duties because they couldn't raise enough support.

Yet, within two months, I managed to secure 50% of the funds necessary to launch *Unveiling Beauty* full-time through monthly partnerships. The journey of raising money was a rollercoaster, fraught with uncertainties, but God's provision was unwavering. Some supporters from that initial ask continue to give to this day, a testament to the enduring faith and generosity that sustains the mission.

In order to raise support, I had to make my vision clear. People do not want to give to a cause that is not going anywhere, so it was critical that I formalize my efforts and projects. *Unveiling Beauty* was not just a name but a mission, so I had to partner with God to map it out. I quickly realized that there were no Saudi leaders ministering to women in the Arabian Gulf. None. At the time of launch, and still to this day, there are no non-profits that are led by Saudi women and specialize in ministering to women of that region.

When I got saved, I thought I was the first Saudi person to ever come to Jesus. In the months that followed, I discovered there were many, many believers and seekers around the world. The truth is, so much of the Middle East is under a veil of secrecy that new Christians and those who are still searching feel very alone. The goal of my ministry is to target these believers and seekers to provide them with community and resources. This is a very important distinction because, as a ministry, we do not engage with combative Muslims who are just looking for an argument or debate. Instead, we engage with those who are searching or those who are in the faith and seeking more.

From the start, we have raised money and divided our

efforts into *projects.* As with any organization, business, or club—these efforts and offerings will change over time. Some ideas work, others don't, some need to die, some need to change, and some need to continue. This is the nature of pioneering and trying new things.

Most of our projects revolve around virtual teaching online, networking, translation work, and retreats for the gathering of women. Our first retreat was in 2018, when a woman in California gave us her house for the weekend. The theme was *Unveiled Emotions,* which created a safe harbor for emotional vulnerability in a way many of the women had never experienced. In the Middle East, saying something as simple as "I'm sad" is simply not an option. Displaying emotion is considered shameful and weak. During this initial retreat, we worked through emotions from a biblical lens and many women found freedom, new insight, and restoration.

We have led Bible translation projects in my own dialect with a team in Al Qatif, and I've traveled from church to church raising awareness and sharing my story. Eventually, we plan to host underground retreats on site throughout the Persian Gulf, modeling the house church in the book of Acts. Plans are also in place to develop a series, which we believe will find its way to major streaming platforms, as well as provide insight through podcasts and print on the restless situations that are plaguing the Middle East.

When the ministry launched, much of my time was

spent speaking in churches. I discovered that one of the biggest challenges of the ministry was getting people to understand the vision and the security needed with a ministry like this. With good intentions, Americans want to promote the ministry and honor the speaker by putting them on the stage. However, I had to be covert and quiet, requesting livestreams to be stopped before taking the stage—knowing the risks involved in the nations we were reaching.

Eventually, I became somewhat disillusioned by the speaking circuit. With a microphone in hand, I felt honored to share about the Middle East, but also felt like a token testimony at times. In a strange way, I felt like I was reduced to a story or segment of a service. Occasionally, I would speak, and after leaving the stage, that was that. There was no sense of community, curiosity, or fellowship beyond just showing up and sharing with a semi-interested crowd. I am more than a story, yet at times it felt like churches were checking a box by having me, and afterward, there was little investment in the relationship itself. It's one thing to be used by God, but it felt wrong to be used by people.

The desire of my heart is to know and be known by my brothers and sisters. I am not interested in leading in order to have followers—I am forging a path and taking territories back for the Kingdom. I am not driven by the need for recognition or to win a popularity contest. I am interested in trailblazing where nobody has gone before. I'm not looking for followers, I'm looking for fellow-trailblazers who share my passion for invitation and adventure.

At times, though, this seemed lacking. I recall one event where a church provided a room for us to do a training on how to reach Muslim women. Many women stayed with question after question, burning with curiosity and passion for reaching the Middle East. Unfortunately, we were kicked out of the room early and had to finish our meeting in the heat outside.

When teaching, I prefer to sit in smaller rooms where questions, feedback, and conversation can happen. For many large churches, the testimony and sermon are more of a monologue, whereas I prefer a *dialogue*.

Does this mean I never speak anymore? Certainly not. I still speak and enjoy it very much. However, I try to only share at a church or a conference if there is a purpose in it that relates directly to the mission of our ministry. If a church is invested in the Middle East or sincerely wants to be a part of what God is doing there, I'll go.

As with any ministry or project, the learning never stops. You try things, some work and others don't; you pivot, grow, and adjust. In those early days, if I could see all the things we would end up doing, I would have been thoroughly overwhelmed. Planting a ministry is much like planting a tree. You start with a simple, single seed—a vision, a mission statement, a name, or a goal. From there, as it is planted, a simple single shoot comes up. Over time, branches form, grow, and stretch, and suddenly the simple seed has become a complex, multi-faceted organization. The growth and development of *Unveiling Beauty* has been no exception.

* * *

In late summer of 2015, on the 11th anniversary of his salvation, Nabeel was diagnosed with stomach cancer and given a 4% chance of survival. It was right around the time that I had launched *Unveiling Beauty*. His battle was quite public as he had become a popular figure in Christian circles by then. I visited him at his home in Houston. He had lost weight and was in severe pain. Saddened by the outlook, he said, "I wonder if my ministry has been fruitful."

I wanted to say, "Um, hello...look at me!" knowing that I was a direct example of the fruitfulness of his ministry. In truth, he had a life ahead of him, a wife, small children, and so much ministry yet to accomplish. However, the timeline he originally had in mind was being cut short, and reconciling this was an emotional challenge, as it would be for anyone.

"I went for a long walk," he said, "and God told me, 'This sickness is for the salvation of your family.'"

His parents, who had previously disowned him, came back when he got sick to express support and sympathy. About a year after his diagnosis, he passed away. Now, any time his family misses him and wants to hear his voice or see him on video, they must turn to his videos and writings, which are all centered around Jesus.

In the weeks, months, and years since Nabeel has gone to be with Jesus, his book, videos, lectures, and sermons have been absorbed by countless souls around the world more times than can be measured. The content he was able to release during his relatively short ministry is a testament to the efficient and powerful grace of God. He was living for a purpose that was greater than himself and greater than his own life. For Muslims coming to Christianity, the idea that God gives us a unique individual purpose is novel and exciting. We have a role to play, a spot to fill, a purpose to carry out.

Networking with Nabeel was an integral part of my salvation and my growth in the faith. As a result, it's no surprise that a big part of my ministry was and is *networking*. With connectedness being high on my strengths list, you might think of me as a redeemed Kingdom *fixer*. I am often given information like, "Hey Sahar, we know a Christian in this city in the Middle East. Do you have a contact for an underground home group they can join?" From there, I work my network and make things happen. This sort of networking, arranging, and dot-connecting has remained a core function of my ministry.

On one such occasion, while living in Irvine, I heard from a ministry partner about a Saudi woman who had escaped Saudi and desperately wanted to end up in America but got held up in Europe. Eventually, through a long set of circumstances, she was stuck in China and needed to find a way to the States. The founder of a local law firm called *Advocates for Faith & Freedom* went to church with the couple I was staying with at the time. Among many things, they help persecuted Christians and asylum seekers from the Middle East.

At the time, a lawyer named Nada Higuera was working at the firm and wanted to meet with me. I went into the meeting simply to connect with an attorney who could help a persecuted Christian in my network. I left the meeting with the start of a lasting friendship. I first noticed Nada's attire. She was well dressed with expensive shoes and a nice dress. I thought, *She is upper class. There's no way she wants to be friends with me.* It's quite funny how we can assess the age, education level, and social class of a person from the first few seconds of meeting them.

As we arranged ourselves at the table, she said, "Don't worry about your friend's case. We'll do that another time. I really want to know *you.*" The conversation began and flowed with ease and joy. Nada and I had very similar backgrounds. She, too, had left the Muslim faith and was in America pursuing a career helping others. She experienced oppression in her upbringing, and I had gone through the same things in Saudi Arabia. In the course of the discussion, it turned out that I lived five minutes from her office.

"Do you have Instagram? I want to be friends with you," she said.

From there, we met up again, and again, and again. We shared worldviews, had deep discussions, and laughed routinely. I discovered her intelligence and wit. She has a sarcastic, dry humor that is infectious. In her work, she is fierce and passionate, having fought and won massive, high-profile cases as a lawyer.

It quickly became clear that we had not met by happenstance but because of the hand of God. There is a threshold that is passed in relationships where an acquaintance becomes a friend, and a friend becomes a best friend.

Nada and I have become so close over the years that we even celebrate our *friendiversary* together each year. God knit our hearts to learn and grow together. It seems that in every season of life, God has us in a similar moment. When I was learning about emotional healing for myself, God was doing the same for her. When I found out why family members of mine behaved in certain ways, she was discovering the same things about hers.

Both of us are called to the healing of women—she through legal support and I through covert ministry. As we are out and about, people often mistake us for sisters. The first time a woman asked, "Are you sisters?" Nada said, "No," and I said, "Yes," at the same time. I said, "We are sisters, blood sisters—by the blood of Jesus." From then on, the answer from both of us has always been *yes*.

Jesus sent them out two by two. Meeting Nada was the start of a lifelong partnership in ministry, truly fulfilling the passage which says, "Two are better than one" (see Ecclesiastes 4:9). Given that I had personally benefited from networking so much in my faith journey, it only made sense that an integral part of my ministry would be offering the same to others.

Unveiling Beauty offers a safe place for Arab women and equips them to embrace their femininity, leverage their gifts, find their true identity in Christ, and walk in the freedom and confidence that is meant for them. Occasionally, I'm in awe of the move of God, the stories I hear, the freedom, and the transformation I see the Holy Spirit working out. This sisterhood, these deep friendships, and the privilege of walking alongside my sisters make my life rich and meaningful. If you haven't met a Middle Eastern sister today, I encourage you to go find her, invite her to your world, and share yours with her. Go find your sister!

A great exchange between Peter and Jesus has marked me and has become my reality. Peter approached Jesus, saying, "'See, we have left everything and followed you.' Jesus said, 'Truly, I say to you, there is no one who has left house or brothers or sisters or mother or father or children or lands, for my sake and for the gospel, who will not receive a hundredfold now in this time, houses and brothers and sisters and mothers and children and lands, with persecutions, and in the age to come eternal life'" (Mark 10:28-30).

CHAPTER ELEVEN

Beyond America

The Global Kingdom of God

"We must be global Christians with a global vision because our God is a global God."

–JOHN STOTT

During a visit to Oklahoma for ministry, a group of people who led an outreach to Muslims encouraged me to set up camp there in the Sooner state. "Come live here, we can do a lot together," they said. While Oklahoma was small, many people with an Arabic background lived there, which made it fertile ground for my new ministry.

The move would provide me with two things: first, a local population of Middle Easterners whom I could reach, and second, a place to anchor as I began the process of being naturalized as an American citizen. As I prayed about it, I heard the Lord saying, "If you don't move, you'll miss the many blessings I have for you here."

A church in Oklahoma sponsored my move and helped with arrangements, even sending a woman to fly out and drive me from Irvine to Oklahoma City. Beyond that, I was offered an office at the church and worked closely with the woman who specialized in ministry to Muslims.

As for the church itself, it was huge. Each service was packed with Oklahomans. They were of the Baptist background, which meant they loved the Bible but tended to place less emphasis on the power of the Holy Spirit—something I was not used to. Some build a church without the Holy Spirit, and they are left with knowledge but no power. Jesus is the power of God and the wisdom of God (see 1 Corinthians 1:24). Jesus builds His Kingdom by the power of the Spirit, so we must establish our churches and ministries likewise. Knowing about God feeds your mind, but transformation is lacking. Knowing God *truly,* through the Spirit, can change us to be like Jesus.

During a mission trip with the church, we had a group of men and a group of women attending. We were scheduled to have a Bible study when I noticed something was off. Women were not allowed to lead. As a result, because the regular leaders were out of town, an eighteen-year-old boy led the group, and it was clear that he did not know what he was doing. Not only that, but women would not speak up, share, or volunteer to pray.

I had an idea and announced it: "Let's divide into two groups, men and women." After separating, women who normally would not speak began to share, and I was able to hear their hearts. They prayed beautifully and had valuable insight to offer. When starting the ministry *Unveiling Beauty,* my aim was to unveil the value of Middle Eastern women who had been oppressed. Unveiling American women was new territory, yet I found that many of the Muslim norms regarding the suppression of female voices were at play here in the Christian church.

Men saw me as being too bold. *How dare I?* I felt like a fish out of water as the only Middle Eastern woman *and* the only one who believed men and women can lead together. Women have valuable input to offer, and by de-platforming them, we deprive ourselves of their insight. Because of this, I often left the church discouraged on Sundays.

When I was a Muslim, I questioned why there were no prophetesses in Islam. In the Bible, I saw the value of women as equal to men. I noted Deborah, Esther, Mary, and other biblical figures who were given leadership, influence, and power. Many women leaving the Muslim faith still question their roles. On more than one occasion, I've heard sentiments like, "Sahar, you're single and doing this ministry without a man's covering?"

There is a line in the film *Gladiator (2000),* where Marcus Aurelius says to his daughter, Lucilla, "If only you had been born a man, what a Caesar you would have made." This mentality was felt by me growing up and felt even more as I broke barriers in my calling. At the end of the day,

I have Jesus. Of course, I have a board, accountability, and I am not a lone ranger female leader. However, I have seen the testimony of my ministry and leadership be a powerful encouragement to single women who have realized they do not need a man in order to follow God. If you want to be married—great, but you don't *have* to in order to fulfill your purpose. The Kingdom of God is not just redemption for me as a human, but empowerment for me as a woman.

While the church in Oklahoma did not necessarily see eye to eye with me on this front, the missions pastor was gifted, prophetic, intellectual, and amazing. To this day, I revisit his sermons as they were formative for me. Nevertheless, I knew that I needed something else in the long term.

I recall praying, "Lord, where are the people on fire? Please lead me to the women on fire for You in this city." Shortly after, I was connected with another ministry called *Sallt* (Salt and Light Leadership Training). Whether you're a doctor, a pastor, a veterinarian, or a waiter, you can be trained by them in leadership. It was a Spirit-driven curriculum that equipped believers to have influence in their respective fields. Whether your background was Baptist, charismatic, Catholic, or something else entirely, you could attend their events and classes to be awakened and empowered.

Through Sallt, I was introduced to a powerful woman named Cynthia Huffmyer. She leads a ministry called *Breakthrough,* and I recall with fondness our three-hour discussion where I shared my life testimony and had deep conversations with her. These talks revolved around hearing God's voice and direction for our lives. God answered my prayer; I had truly found the women on fire.

God's word came to pass; in Oklahoma, I truly did experience many of the blessings that He had for me. There, after much time and heartache, I met my counselor, Sheila. She is godly, strong, and understands my culture. Sheila became a pillar of strength and wisdom in my life and has helped me understand my inner child, my role in the family, and how to deal with my difficult, narcissistic mother. Oklahoma was proving to be a hub of divine appointments.

Nothing we go through will be wasted by God. Whether positive, negative, or neutral, God is able to redeem and utilize all of our experiences to further His purposes in our lives. God can turn shortcomings into overcomings and failures into successes. Paul wrote, "And we know that for those who love God all things work together for good, for those who are called according to his purpose" (Romans 8:28). At each phase of my ministry, I was collecting experiences— good and bad—that all contributed to where I am today and where I am going in the future.

During my time in Oklahoma, I passed a very significant date in my life. For some, 2020 was a year marked by life changes, lockdowns, and isolation. It was a time of upheaval and uncertainty. For me, I arrived at my 36th birthday. It was a birthday that spurred reflection unlike any other because my own father did not live to see past his 36th year.

I recall talking to one of my younger brothers and playing a game called *Where Do We Begin?* by Esther Perel. The cards gave prompts and questions to encourage conversation. One of them asked, "What would you ask your parents if you could ask them anything?"

Nearly without hesitation, my brother said, "I would ask Dad, *How did you do it?* He had a house, a career, a family, and had fought through physical limitations and a crazy upbringing. How did he pull that off?"

I would love to hear his answer to that question as well. In truth, he did *so* much in such a short time. As I passed through the door of my 36th birthday, I realized what a short time it truly was. God began to speak to me about how I was picking up the ministry where my father left off. He had set me up, and now I was to run to the finish line to continue my father's calling.

The seed of curiosity toward the Christian faith that my father had planted in me had since been watered, sustained, and had blossomed into a heartfelt passion for Jesus and the ministry of the gospel. The fire in my heart to share the love of God and to be a light has not faded but grown. I live with a passion for those God has called me to and a burning desire to continue my father's legacy.

I had planned to stay in Oklahoma until my immigration process was completed. Because my case was based there, that is where I would have to appear for biometrics, interviews, swearing in, and so forth. However, a few years into my time there, I visited Dallas to connect with a friend. While there, I had a vivid dream from the Lord that I must move to this city.

Upon waking up, I registered that it was from God, but also felt like it was implausible. My lease in Oklahoma was not yet fulfilled, and wiggling out of that would usually be huge money. In prayer, God put it on my heart that the people who owned the building also had buildings in Dallas, and He assured me that the move would be easy. I reached out to the property manager and told them my situation.

"Yeah," he replied, "we have apartments in Dallas. Just pay us $200 and pay the other office a $200 transfer fee, and you'll be good to go." With the small investment of $400, I could make the move and then just drive three hours north to Oklahoma City when it was time to be sworn in as a citizen.

It was an amazingly smooth transition. Dallas pulsed with ministry and gospel-centered output. The sprawling city headquartered so many ministries, non-profits, and churches that I felt like I was right in the middle of the gospel hub. While the transition was smooth, it has been difficult to walk the path of a nomad. My entire adult life has been a transition from one country to the next and from one state to the next. I may be based out of Dallas for now, but who knows where God might call me next? The networking has been incredible, and practically speaking, DFW offers great international flights compared to Oklahoma City. I truly feel at home in the community of believers in Dallas.

Six years after applying for asylum and Covid delaying my immigration process, I made the drive up north from Dallas to be naturalized as an American citizen. A sense of permanence was in the room as I passed security and entered the spot where I would be sworn in. With one hand in the air, I repeated the following oath:

> "I hereby declare, on oath, that I absolutely and entirely renounce and abjure all allegiance and fidelity to any foreign prince, potentate, state, or sovereignty, of whom or which I have heretofore been a subject or citizen; that I will support and defend the Constitution and laws of the United States of America against all enemies, foreign and domestic; that I will bear true faith and allegiance to the same; that I will bear arms on behalf of the United States when required by the law; that I will perform noncombatant service in the Armed Forces of the United States when required by the law; that I will perform work of national importance under civilian direction when required by the law; and that I take this obligation freely, without any mental reservation or purpose of evasion; so help me God."

Permanent citizenship meant a wealth of potential opportunities, from education to travel and employment. I couldn't help but recognize the gravity of the event, knowing I was gaining the most sought-after citizenship in the world. The American passport would grant me the ability to travel more freely and safely around the world, a treasure for someone who has experienced severe limitations on movement.

* * *

As a Saudi Christian, I did notice a troubling trend in the American church. For many, American citizenship seems to be the equivalent of Kingdom citizenship. I became increasingly uncomfortable with the tight link between American politics and the outlook of the church. I was not a Christian because I became an American citizen, and I am not an American citizen because I became a Christian.

I found myself navigating a complex landscape of faith and identity. Within many churches and circles, I became aware of a pressure to conform, to become an "American Christian," even though my roots were and are firmly planted in the Arab world. I wondered, how much of American Christianity is *cultural* but not *biblical*? This struggle has led me to a broader critique of how American Christianity often centers itself as the heart of God's Kingdom, sometimes neglecting the global and diverse nature of Christ's body. After all, America is not the Kingdom of God.

Let's make no mistake, I love this country, and I am eternally grateful for the opportunities I have been afforded here. The United States has been an integral part of God's plan in delivering me from the oppression of the Middle East. In fact, my critique is primarily toward the church rather than the state. In observing American Christianity, I've noticed a concerning trend where many look to politicians as saviors, believing that the right leader will bring about a godly nation. While voting and having a voice in a free country are vitally important, our ultimate allegiance must be to Jesus, not a political figure. Our citizenship is ultimately in heaven, and while we should emphasize godly impact within the politisphere, we must rest our hope in Christ alone and retain a global vision.

Reflecting on the biblical narrative, it's striking how John's vision on the island of Patmos, which outlines the end times, is notably silent on America. You won't find passages in Revelation detailing America's electoral college or how a single campus revival is going to usher in Christ's second coming. Yet, many American Christians act as if God's eschatological timeline revolves around their country alone. They ignore the vibrant growth of Christianity in places like China, North Korea, and Iran, where believers multiply underground despite severe persecution. The focus on American revival overlooks the global nature of God's work. Prolific election prophecies often reflect this misguided focus, distracting from the true work of the Kingdom, which transcends national borders.

Because many in the States view "Americanism" and

"Christianity" as one and the same, they fail to understand those of other cultures and backgrounds. There is a prevalent misunderstanding of the Muslim world within American Christianity. I have heard some Christians commend Muslims for their devout prayer practices, saying things like, "At least the Muslims are dedicated to daily prayer! We as Christians should be that committed also!"

In truth, this view is superficial. These Islamic practices are driven by fear and social pressure rather than genuine, fervent love for God. It isn't a fiery passion but a fear of hell. The oppressive nature of this religious adherence is overlooked, as is the prevalence of a double life among many Muslims—outwardly conforming while secretly rebelling. In my experience, there were families who outwardly adhered to Islamic norms but behaved differently abroad, away from societal scrutiny. For example, Bahrain served as a sort of escape from Saudi Arabia's stringent regulations, with movie theaters, alcohol, and less restrictive environments. So no, a "devout Muslim" may not be all that devout internally. Just like in Christianity, there are swaths of people who are simply going through the motions.

If a Muslim ministry were to try to reach Americans, a direct translation of written materials probably would not excel. Why? Because there is an understanding of American culture that would be required to be effective. Likewise, when American ministries aim to reach the Middle East, there is an understanding of culture, communication styles, attitudes, norms, and a grasp on how information is consumed that is required.

Often, American discipleship models reflect American culture more than the universal gospel. For instance, material translated for use in the Middle East frequently fails because it doesn't account for cultural differences. Let's be clear, God loves America and wants to use it for His purposes, but America is not the direct reflection of the Kingdom of God. Therefore, we must avoid imposing our systems and culture on others and instead become all things to all people, as Paul taught.

Here is an example: In my ministry, I emphasize interactive teaching, knowing that oral tradition and dialogue are deeply valued in my home Arab culture. Long lectures and extensive written materials are less effective in reaching hearts and minds. This approach reflects the broader principle that God created us differently, and our methods must adapt to these differences.

Americans may prefer a Sunday morning monologue as opposed to a Middle Eastern style dialogue, and that is okay. We simply have to recognize that *what* we share does not change, but *how* we share it does. Western Christianity must embrace a more global perspective, recognizing that the Kingdom of God is far broader and more diverse than any one nation. Of course, I am not the first one to critique Western philosophy on missions, but these insights are worth unpacking. We should celebrate the unique ways God is working around the world and learn from each other, rather than trying to conform everyone to a single cultural expression of faith.

Think of the Kingdom as an upside-down funnel. It starts narrow (see Matthew 7:13) but then widens into a broad expression that can meet each culture and nation where it is. The problem is, many view the Kingdom as a right-side up funnel, where you take in everyone through a broad opening and then conform them to a single culture.

Perhaps my sensitivity to this comes from my background in Islam. The Muslim faith is centered in the Middle East and demands conformity. Passages must be read in Arabic with proper pronunciation, and Islamic garb is mandated no matter where you are in the world. I know what it means to allow a culture to define and enforce a faith, and it would be heartbreaking to see a similar tragedy among American Christians.

I should note that cultural misunderstandings are not limited to people in the States. Growing up, I was taught that Americans were morally corrupt, with Christians being particularly loose and immoral. This perception was reinforced during my time at Chico State, a known party school, where the behavior of many students confirmed my biases. I saw a Christian confession on one hand and sleeping around and overindulging in alcohol on the other. I've since learned that these views were overly simplistic and that there are many aspects of the Western world that are misunderstood in the Middle East—and vice versa. Most of the Christians who lived recklessly were just nominal Christians who didn't actually reflect the gospel. The same thing is true with the hell, fire, and brimstone street preachers I had encountered before my salvation. They may have worn a Christian label, but they did not represent the actual heart of Jesus.

Without question, America and its people are a beacon of freedom and a hub of missions that have dispensed liberty, the gospel, and truth to the world. Nevertheless, we must remain on guard against the easy temptation to allow our culture to shape the gospel rather than letting the gospel shape our culture. By acknowledging these realities, we may embrace a more effective global view of Christianity and better fulfill our mission to be the body of Christ in a diverse and interconnected world. Unlike the kingdoms and cultures of this world that come and go, we are laboring within "a kingdom which cannot be shaken" (Hebrews 12:28).

* * *

A new passport meant new chances to travel. Fifteen years had passed since landing in Washington, D.C., and I had yet to return to Saudi Arabia. As the ministry grew and became established, I did the majority of my outreach digitally, yet the time came for me to get back to Arabia with boots on the ground, so to speak.

After several layovers and ample time in the air, the sunny, sandy slopes of the Middle Eastern landscape came into view as I touched down at King Abdulaziz International Airport. As I exited the plane and made my way onto the jet bridge, I was officially on Saudi soil without my veil for the first time since I was a little girl. It was not just my appearance that had changed, but *I* had changed. I was not only an American citizen now, but a citizen of the Kingdom of heaven.

As I made my way through customs, I entered with a U.S. passport completely untethered from the past. I've been told I have a very "international" look—being mistaken as Hispanic, Italian, Persian, and more. As far as they were concerned, I was a newcomer to Saudi Arabia, raised in the West. Even if they saw my birthplace of Saudi Arabia in the fine print of my passport, they would likely assume I was born in Saudi to a Western family who had lived there for work.

Saudi Arabia viewed me as a new person and, in a sense, I viewed Saudi Arabia as a new land. The things I did not appreciate before I left, I was now soaking up. I came with a fresh understanding of my homeland. I was not just walking into the desert of my upbringing, but I was traversing the very land of Arabia where the Apostle Paul was discipled for several years, "...nor did I go up to Jerusalem to those who were apostles before me; but I went to Arabia, and returned again to Damascus. Then after three years I went up to Jerusalem" (Galatians 1:17-18).

I was not just visiting family and enjoying the old foods I used to love. I was seeing the Sinai Arabian wilderness where the children of Israel wandered for 40 years. In fact, there is a big mountain in Saudi that is charred on the top where many scholars believe Moses met with God to receive the Ten Commandments[17]. Even the locals will acknowledge that. The split rock of Horeb lies in the northwestern part of the country, showcasing the very point where water gushed from the rock that Moses split.

As I visited my hometown, reminiscing with those I had not seen in ages, I could not help but think of the scenes from the Bible right in their backyard. To me, Saudi Arabia was no longer a monolith of Shias and Sunnis but a museum of the Scriptures. I envision a day when the nation is swept with the gospel and masses come to Christ. When such things happen, a passion will arise amongst Middle Easterners like we have never seen before. Why? Because when they walk outside, they are beholding the very landscape where the Bible played out. My people are worshipers! Once they know the true God, who alone is worthy of worship, they worship Him with everything they have.

---

17. Froelich, Paula. *Archaeologist claims Mount Sinai found in Saudi Arabia.* October 2, 2021. https://nypost.com/2021/10/02/archaeologist-claims-mount-sinai-found-in-saudi-arabia/

Saudi Arabia has come a long way since its founding less than 100 years ago. It transformed from a primitive desert full of tribes engaged in strange hybrid worship to an Islamic theocracy. Shortly after its inception during the boom of the automobile, the discovery of vast oil reserves under the sand made the kingdom a major economic player in global affairs. Middle Eastern skylines have changed from the hot sun setting over endless dunes to tall, world-class skyscrapers and perfectly manicured streets.

For so long, Middle Eastern governments have had a reputation for corruption, double standards, and waste. While the citizens of Saudi are sent to jail for possessing alcohol, the rulers import it from Bahrain and throw extravagant parties. A person in government once told me that it's not uncommon for a Saudi official to send a helicopter to Lebanon to pick up food and bring it back to the palace.

It's no secret that power and money have the ability to corrupt those who have them. As the nation changes, though, they are becoming more democratic and offering liberties to the people, which I pray will provide balance to the power structures. As Saudi Arabia becomes less isolated and more involved in European and American affairs, the impact of the West is evident. At the time of this writing, the crown prince, Mohammed bin Salman (MBS), is the youngest ruler to ever take the throne in Saudi. He is quite progressive and westernized in his thinking and even rolled out what he has coined the *2030 plan.*[18]

The plan includes several key initiatives aimed at reducing the country's dependence on oil, diversifying the economy, and developing public service sectors like health, education, infrastructure, recreation, and even tourism. Basically, it is following the European blueprint and becoming a more friendly player on the global front. As MBS says, "The Middle East can be the 'New Europe.'"[19]

Beyond infrastructure and economics, the vision promotes cultural activities, women's rights, and social reforms to modernize Saudi society and increase participation in the workforce. Ultimately, Vision 2030 wants to transform Saudi Arabia into a global investment powerhouse and a strategic hub connecting Asia, Europe, America, and Africa.

To pull this off, the crown prince knows the nation must look more like the West and less like the stereotypical Middle East. Women have already been given far more freedom and authority compared to when I left. The international scholarship program effectively sent out Saudi students to be educated in Europe and America. When they came back to work in Saudi corporations and the government, they im-

---

18. Kingdom of Saudi Arabia. "Vision 2030." Accessed November 7, 2024. https://www.vision2030.gov.sa/en.
19. Arab News, "Saudi Arabia Celebrates 88th National Day," *Arab News*, October 18, 2018, accessed February 10, 2025, https://www.arabnews.com/node/1393491/saudi-arabia.

ported European ideas of equality and economic opportunity for all, regardless of gender.

Women are now favored in employment and even working in high government positions. Some say there is a bit of an over-correction that's taking place, where a man will lose out on jobs to a woman regardless of qualification. Other fundamentalists are upset about the progress, wishing for an old iteration of Saudi with little to no opportunity for women.

Ultimately, these steps will not only change Saudi Arabia but will change how the world views it as well. During my trip back to the homeland, witnessing these changes, I could not help but contextualize them with my newfound Christian faith. I began to think about the finances generated in the Middle East and how this could impact the spread of the gospel. There was a time when Northern Europe was powerful but pagan, and after becoming Christianized, it became civil, free, and has been a positive force for the Kingdom of God. I wonder what the Middle East might look like in 100 years? What might Saudi Arabia be doing for the gospel in 500 years, should the Lord tarry? How will this wealth be sanctified for God's purposes? Are we finishing the work Paul started in Arabia (see Galatians 1:17)?

We have recently launched a project based on this vision of reconciliation and transformation, drawing inspiration from Scripture. It's rooted in the allegory of Hagar and Sarah (see Galatians 4:22-27), and the project reminds us of

God's promise of freedom—a promise that I believe extends even to the land of Saudi Arabia. Isaiah 60 paints a prophetic picture of Arabia's wealth being sanctified and flowing toward Jerusalem in preparation for the Second Coming of Christ, "...so that people may bring you the wealth of the nations." This vision compels us to act now, working for reconciliation and unity among believers.

Our project seeks to connect Arabs from Muslim backgrounds with Messianic Jewish people, breaking down centuries of hostility and building bridges of understanding and love. Through online teaching, prayer, and in-person gatherings, this initiative calls for fellowship between these two groups, helping them embrace their shared faith in Christ. By creating opportunities for healing and forgiveness, I believe this project will not only change lives but also fulfill God's prophetic plan for the region.

I recognize that the Christian population in Israel is relatively small compared to Jews and Muslims—about 1.9%, mostly Arab Christians, compared to 73.5% Jews and 18.1% Muslims. Still, our presence matters. We carry a love for both sides, and many of us long to be a bridge—faithfully standing in the middle, praying for healing, and speaking peace. Even among Christians, there is often separation between Arab Christ-followers and Messianic Jews, split by culture, politics, and years of misunderstanding.

Christ-followers from Muslim backgrounds who support Israel do exist. It's a perspective rarely seen and often misunderstood. We walk a lonely road, rejected by our families, and heartbreakingly, even by the Arabic Church. Still, we remain. We are here—holding the tension, standing in the gap, believing that reconciliation is possible.

I want the project to actively embody Paul's words in Ephesians 2:14-16—breaking down walls of hostility and creating one new family in Christ. Together, Arab and Jewish women can demonstrate the unity and peace that only God can provide, pointing to the ultimate reconciliation of all things through the cross (see Colossians 1:19-20).

Within the borders of my homeland, bouncing from house to house, covertly encouraging believers and reconnecting with family, I knew that God was not done with the Middle East, but that His plans were just getting started.

CHAPTER TWELVE

God Stands with Israel, So Do I!

Embracing a Bold Path to Peace for Israel, Judea, and Beyond.

"For I will take you out of the nations; I will gather you from all the countries and bring you back into your own land." –Ezekiel 36:24

I was walking in a very dark place—surrounded by a black, unwelcoming landscape. When I looked out onto the horizon to my right and to my left, I could see nothing but pitch black darkness. The only light available was Jesus, who was walking in front of me, illuminating the path ahead. "Where are we?" I asked the Lord.

"We are in Bethlehem. It's dark here, Sahar, and I am calling you to be a light."

The moment He said this, I began to glow with the same bright light that He was emitting. I woke up from the dream knowing that Bethlehem, in the land of Judea, the very place of Jesus' birth, is part of modern-day Palestine, and that God had a calling for me in that region. This was six years ago.

In the days, weeks, and months that came after the dream, I pressed into what the Lord was calling me to do. I would seek, inquire, and ask God to open doors. Like a bird that followed me around from day to day, flying over my head and swooping across my mind, the thoughts of this region seemed to loom and linger. While I did not know *when* or *how* my ministry would unfold in that area, I knew an assignment was ahead of me, and I brimmed with anticipation.

My history with the region of Israel and Palestine goes all the way back to childhood. In school growing up, we had a number of Palestinian kids in class, and they routinely said, with anger, "The Jews kicked us out!" At that time, the Saudi government offered passports to massive waves of displaced Palestinians. It's the only time in history when this occurred, and it is still an unprecedented action.

I treated Palestinians differently than the others and always exhibited much more compassion and empathy for them as a people. This soft spot has remained for my entire life and increased all the more after I came to Jesus. Even before I was saved, a Palestinian Christian named Elias from Beit Jala | بيت جالا (near Bethlehem) shared the gospel with me, and after launching the ministry, I became best friends with Nada, who was originally from Palestine as well.

The region had such a rich biblical heritage but was now a place of conflict, strife, tension, and extreme political turmoil. This conflict is not the conflict of our generation. It is the conflict of *generations* that has continued for far too long. To make my position even more complicated, I also had a heart that swelled with love for the Jewish people. As mentioned earlier in the book, the Middle Eastern airwaves are dominated by antisemitic propaganda that brainwashes the Islamic mind into thinking that the totality of the world's problems can be blamed on .2% of the world's population—namely, the Jews.

I could not and cannot stomach such unfounded hate. I recall a pleasant friendship I had with a Jewish girl from Israel whom I met at a coffee shop in Boulder. I think back to the pleasant Jewish people I encountered at the Children of Abraham gatherings. And now, as a Christian, I have a biblical point of view toward Israel, which reaffirms my love for them all the more.

Because of a long-held love for this region and people on both sides of the divide, I wanted to see the area with my own eyes. To be on the ground meant I might be able to reconcile the differing opinions and offer the solution of Jesus to both camps. Where two Abrahamic faiths fight, the third and true Abrahamic faith—Christianity—brings peace.

I had been sitting on my dream about this region for several years when, out of the blue, God spoke to me on the topic once again. It was December of 2022, and I was driving to a friend's house for a Christmas gathering. I listened to *Mary Did You Know?* performed by an Arab who lives in Israel, an American Christian girl, and a Jewish girl singing their parts in Arabic, English, and Hebrew. *I loved it.* The very atmosphere of my car bustled with faith. I had a ministry trip planned for Sweden in February the following year. I thought it would be my first trip overseas as an American Citizen, but as I listened to the song, I heard the Holy Spirit tell me that I would be going to Israel first.

"When?" I asked.

"In two days," I heard back.

As someone who is quite organized by nature, I don't plan a dinner party with just two days' notice, much less an international trip. After arriving at the Christmas party, my mind raced. Focusing on the gift exchange, small talk, and the Middle Eastern BBQ on the table proved impossible. Israel and my trip to it in 48 hours were the only things on my mind. I left early and called a certain friend who came to mind, asking her to pray with me because booking it with such short notice seemed crazy—irresponsible, even.

After praying, she sensed that the Lord was in on the assignment and said, "Sahar, I know you will go. This is God." Then, unprovoked, she sent me $4,000 to pay for the trip. Humbled and amazed, I asked a friend to arrange the travel and tickets. Another friend came over to pray with me. As we sat together, a prophetic grace came into the room and she declared, "On this trip, people are going to receive you with joy. I see you bringing joy to the land from house to house."

The night before leaving, I could not sleep. For several weeks leading up to this, I would wake up saying the word "manal | منال," which means "desire" in Arabic. That night, I had an encounter with an angel, and within me, I knew that the angel's name was *Manal* | منال and that this angel would accompany me on my trip to Israel. I received a download from heaven that another angel would join me, named *Amel*| أمل, which means *hope*. It was a sweet reminder from the Holy Spirit that what He is calling me to do might be dangerous and abnormal, but He has assigned angels to protect me, to bring me favor, to push out the darkness, and to usher in the light of God.

Angels are often linked to your calling and assignment. In Scripture, they are described as, "Ministering spirits sent out to serve for the sake of those who are to inherit salvation" (Hebrews 1:14). I knew that *desire* and *hope* would be stirred up within those I was serving. These encounters gave me a fresh sense of security, peace, and purpose in the trip. So often we rush God when He gives us a dream or a vision. However, God's timing is just as important as God's assignment. I had waited half a decade from the time I dreamed of walking in the darkness of Bethlehem to the time I was on a flight to Tel Aviv. The wait was worth it, and the trip would prove that to be so.

* * *

When entering Israel, you must pass through two areas of customs, and they are notoriously stringent with foreigners. Upon landing, a border agent approached and began speaking to me in Hebrew, assuming I was Israeli. Because he thought I was a local, I skipped one checkpoint altogether and was pushed ahead. While I had an American passport, I was concerned about entry, knowing that my birthplace of Saudi Arabia was on the document. Because Israel and Saudi Arabia have no diplomatic ties, travel for people from these regions has proved difficult, often requiring extra regulatory steps and interrogation.

As I approached the final checkpoint, I listened to the conversation ahead of me. A Russian lady named Nadia was talking to the border agent. She looked like a typical Eastern European with blonde hair and blue eyes.

"Why do you have an Arab name!?" the man demanded to know.

"I'm from Russia," she said nervously.

They then quickly pulled her aside for further questioning, simply for having an Arabic name. I wondered how the Holy Spirit would intervene as I approached, knowing I not only had an Arabic name, but an Arabic look and a passport with Saudi Arabia in the details.

"Why are you here?" he asked, looking at my passport.

"I'm a Christian, coming to visit the Holy Land," I replied.

"And how long are you staying?"

"Eight days."

"Welcome to Israel."

And just like that, *I was in.*

Forty-eight hours before, I was singing in my car on the way to a Christmas party in Dallas. Now, I was waiting for a taxi in Tel Aviv. I heard two guys speculating in Arabic, "Where is she from? She looks Arab but also doesn't." I resemble an Arab but don't carry myself like one, which caused the confusion.

One of the men approached me, "Where are you from?" he asked.

"Half European, half Arab," I fibbed. As a citizen of the world, I could fit in anywhere, and the last thing I needed was to raise attention with a curious local. I hopped in a cab and told the driver which hotel in Nazareth I was staying in.

"Stay in Tel Aviv," he said, "I'll introduce you to my wife, you can stay in our guest room."

"Thank you, but I have friends in Nazareth," I replied.

He shot back, "Nazareth is full of Arabs. They're not nice people."

Clearly, he thought I was European, and not an Arab myself. Nevertheless, he dropped me off and for the first two days of the trip, I did not schedule to meet with anyone. I opted instead to walk around the region, pray, and observe the territory with God. While I adjusted to jet lag, I made my way into cafes, taking in the sights and sounds, in awe that

God had fulfilled His word to me so quickly. Open doors are often discussed in Christendom. How do we find the doors? How do we get them to open? For me, the pattern has been simple: assignments usually start with a nudge from God or a spontaneous desire that I know I did not place there myself. Then it may be followed by a dream or vision. Then, with time, doors simply open as I remain willing to enter.

We don't have to scramble to find keys or strive to pry open the door. When our hearts are tender and patient, God will open doors that no man can shut (see Revelation 3:7). As I walked the limestone streets of Nazareth, I felt I had stepped through an open door and that this door would remain open for many years. Tears came to my eyes easily on the trip, and a tenderness overwhelmed me. I sensed God's pleasure over Israel and His sadness as well. Jesus wept over Jerusalem (see Luke 19:41), and I believe those tears continue to flow through His body on earth. The tension is so real in that region, you would have to be spiritually deaf not to feel it. I didn't sleep much during the trip due to the busy schedule and the surge of adrenaline and newness.

The first night there, I woke up to the Muslim Prayer call (Athan | أذان), which I had not heard for almost 12 years. The sounds of the prayer call saddened me and reminded me of what Jesus saved me from. I played worship music and started to pray over the city, that Jesus would have mercy and bring salvation to Muslims.

After those initial few days, the ministry and networking began. A couple of years prior, in 2020, I had started a podcast for Unveiling Beauty. I received a message from a Palestinian man named Nizar, who was a frequent listener, telling me that he ran a radio program called *Voice of Hope* in Israel, which aimed to share the gospel with Arabic-speaking locals. He was young, had great vision, and told me they would love to syndicate my podcast to their radio audience as they had never before platformed a Saudi woman encouraging others in the faith.

This was the start of a budding friendship and ministry connection. I sent him all of my recordings, and he would broadcast them throughout the Middle East. For some time, I had told him about my dream of coming to Israel. He was amazed by my love for the nation, as most of his fellow Palestinians felt the opposite. In fact, he avoided the word "Israel" altogether, opting to use the less divisive Christian phrase *Holy Land*.

Naturally, when I found out I would be coming, he was one of the first people I called. He immediately connected me with his church, and from there, my schedule for the trip filled up quickly. It turns out, God had been planning the trip's logistics well ahead of time. The Lord opened many doors to natural conversations with locals. When people would talk to me, we would exchange spiritual conversations, creating opportunities to encourage others.

When I began connecting with the local believers, they would warn me, "Be careful with your sharing. You're not in

America anymore." I was fine and felt secure praying and being vulnerable with others. I felt at home, and already I didn't want to leave.

A few days into the trip, I went to the Arabic church in Israel. Upon meeting the pastor a few days before service, he said, "You're a Saudi, a Christian, and you love Israel. This is huge. You need to be on stage. Many Arabs are afraid to share the gospel with fellow Muslims. I will be handing you the mic on Sunday for our service."

I had not gone with the intention of speaking, but when the door opened, I once again stepped in. As I took the stage that Sunday, the Holy Spirit spoke to me, "You will come back and live here one day." I was not surprised as I felt at home from the start. From the pulpit, my testimony flowed from my lips, and I felt a powerful anointing, knowing I was sharing, inspired by the same Jesus who walked and taught and healed in the very region I was standing. The very air that carried His voice through this region 2,000 years ago was the same air carrying mine in that moment. The opportunity was a divine appointment, as many in the congregation met me after the service, shared their stories, and opened their homes to me.

One woman said, "You're in our country and you're staying at a hotel? No. You're coming to stay with us." They took me in and offered her kid's bedroom for me to stay in. The lady and I sat and talked until the early hours of the morning. The husband quipped, "I'm jealous—my wife doesn't stay up late, and here you are talking until 3 am."

It was a relational whirlwind, and I didn't want to leave. I went from house to house, hearing amazing stories and sharing my own. It felt like one carefully constructed God-appointment after another, and I could feel my heart being knit to the people. We ate falafel, fresh hummus, halva, and shawarma, washing it down with coffee and tea.

The mother of Nizar was a well of grace and truth. Despite being illiterate, she knew the Bible front to back from listening to it on audio daily. I sat amazed at her story of salvation after a miraculous encounter with the Lord and the grace that swept through her family. They walked in the presence of the Lord in a way that was tangible. The Bible describes that we should provoke the Jewish people to jealousy through our union with God (see Romans 11:11), and the believers I encountered in Israel were certainly occupying that role.

Most ministry efforts in this region are targeted at a particular people group. Some travel to Jerusalem to minister to the Jews, while others travel into Palestine to share with them. In my case, there were two flames in my heart that burned for each. After my experience in the Arab Christian church in Israel, it was time to visit a Palestinian Christian church.

* * *

If you do not believe that Israel is blessed based on Scripture, it is hard to deny that it is blessed based on the landscape. The hot, harsh desert meets its end where Israel begins. Within its borders, you find cool lagoons and lush green palm trees. Mediterranean vegetation abounds with cypress trees, olives, and dates. Just outside of Israel, however, the geography is less inviting.

As I crossed into Palestine, it was a sad scene. Dirt and dust clung to everything. I noted children begging for money and a depressed look that plagued nearly every face. The economy of Palestine is far worse than that of Israel, with the average salary being only a third of what you would earn in Israel.

The geopolitics of the region are complex. The disparity in quality of life between Palestinians and Israelis has only served to reinforce the longstanding bitterness that is held toward the Jewish people. Sadly, these divides are not isolated to Jews and Palestinians and random onlookers from around the world; I found the divide also exists within the Christian churches in the area.

On one occasion during my trip, I was meeting with a Palestinian pastor friend *in* Palestine over lunch. I had some Palestinian friends who were living in Israel who were going to cross over to join and eat with us. The pastor seemed put off right away and asked, "Are they living in Israel?"

"Yes, but they're Palestinian," I responded.

"No, they're not Palestinian. If they were, they would come here and suffer with us."

"They're Christians...believers like us," I rebutted. I thought, surely he will recognize them as brothers and sisters in Christ?

"No," he said, and abruptly got up to leave—refusing to meet with them. He saw them as betrayers and nothing more. I was startled. I began to see that the conflict there is more than a turf war. It's more than an age-old fight over property. It is spiritual, theological, cultural, and deeply rooted in the identities of those who live there. Sadly, in some cases, not even common faith in Jesus is enough to bridge the divide for those with a special sort of stubbornness.

I could not understand it. After getting saved, I had met multiple Palestinian Christians who expressed utter disdain and even hate toward Israel. I even met Christians from other parts of the Middle East, like Lebanon, Syria, Iraq, and Jordan, who felt the same way. As a growing believer, this confused me. I could see in the Bible that God *loves* Israel. Why hate what God loves? Beyond that, Romans 11 is clear that we have been grafted into God's family. How could we be so prideful to reject the family we have been adopted into through the New Covenant?

There *is* a Palestinian church in Nazareth that invites Messianic Jews to speak and has bridged the divide. These examples of godly unity are deeply encouraging. However, the antisemitism is apparent both in and out of the church, which grieves my heart. Antisemitism is the greatest deception in our time. It will show who is on God's side and who is not; it is the separation of the sheep from the goats (see Matthew 25:32-33). The covenant God has with Israel is irrevocable.

I found Israel to be very democratic and Western in terms of freedom and generosity, whereas in other parts of the Middle East, there is a suffocating sense of control at play. Muslims around the world seem to think that Israel is just pointing its gun at every Muslim within their borders, eager to pull the trigger. The truth is, Muslims can freely and openly worship within Israel. There are over 400 mosques inside the small Israeli borders. Now let's flip that idea around. Can you imagine a synagogue in Palestine? Even one of them? Of course not. There are very few places of free public worship for Jews throughout the Middle East. The UAE has made an exception with the Moses Ben Maimon Synagogue, which opened in 2023 as a result of the Abraham Accords Peace Agreement signed in 2020. My heart's desire is to see churches and synagogues all throughout the Arabian Peninsula and the Middle East.

While I love to see this sort of progress, these regions still have a long way to go. The question of who is being tyrannical and bullying can be easily observed. Turkey just recently acknowledged the 100-year anniversary of the fall of the Ottoman Empire, saying that we again need such a caliphate to reign and dispense Islam. This sort of thinking is not limited to the Middle East, but Muslims in the West are also friendly to the idea of an invading government and bringing Islam to power through politics.

Israel is unique in that it's the one place in the Middle East where the three Abrahamic faiths converge, and they all produce different things. For Israelis, being Jewish is two things: it is a race and a religion. It is worship and genetics. While we can discuss their hard-hearted rejection of Jesus as Messiah, we must also acknowledge that they have not gone out of their way to establish a tyrannical theocracy. In fact, most Jews are not interested in any sort of Kingdom outreach at all. On the Muslim front, however, you have an ideology that is driven by conversion through force. History is clear: Where Islam has reigned, the blood of innocents has flowed.

Then we arrive at the third Abrahamic faith in the region: Christianity. Without the help of nations that adhere to Christian principles, Israel would have been without aid and support in conflict after conflict. The gospel itself is a dispenser of peace, joy, love, kindness, goodness, faithfulness, gentleness, and self-control. While it is outspoken, it is not coercive or forceful. It is a fierce and passionate invitation to those near and far to come to the merciful feet of Jesus.

While there, I saw a vision of Christ on the throne in Jerusalem. As I looked, groups and groups of people were coming from all over, and each was dressed in the same color. They had different instruments, singing and praising Him. Flowing from God's throne were different languages and dialects I had never heard before. I saw a glimpse of what was going to happen in Jerusalem as God's people return to the King.

There is much debate over the end times and how the return of Jesus will play out. Some guarantee a pre-trib rapture, while others accept nothing but a post-trib timeline. Some are preterist while others are partial-preterists, dispensationalists, postmillennialists, amillennialists, and so on. No matter where you fall in your opinion of the end times, what most of us can agree on is that the faith of the Middle East has a lot to do with it. This begs the question: What is our role? Given the wild geo-political events that are happening, questions arise: What side do I take? How can I minister effectively? What is the actual history in that region?

Being a former Muslim raised in the Middle East, having a heart for the Jewish people, and now a Christian living in the West—I feel I can share a diverse perspective on the Israel/Palestine conflict that is objective, fair, and ultimately has the heart of God at its core.

When it comes to viewing and responding to the Middle Eastern conflict, *balance* is critical. After getting saved, I did not understand the significance of the Jewish people and Israel. Many Arab Christians find themselves in a similar boat. They and many Western Christians have bought into something called *replacement theology*. This teaches that Christians have superseded and replaced the Jewish people as God's chosen. It ignores the fact that we have been *grafted* into the covenant as adopted children (see Romans 11:17) and instead teaches that Israel has no prophetic significance. Some even view the biblical Israel as completely separate from the modern Israeli state. For Muslims coming to Christianity, they need to be saved from two things: first, the huge deception of Islam, and second, a hatred for Israel.

Christians in the West who adopt replacement theology may be surprised to learn that this is exactly what Muslims espouse as well. Muslims claim that the Quran replaced the Bible and that this replaced the messages of the Jews and Christians. In truth, God is a covenant God and a covenant keeper. His covenant with the Jews is beautiful, personal, and we get to be grafted in. To separate yourself from the Jewish people is to separate yourself from the nutrients and benefits of the roots that we have been grafted into.

For me, Romans 11 was a critical text for seeing the continued significance of Israel. Unfortunately, many Arab believers tend to think that the Jewish people can be categorized the same way we might categorize Hindus or Buddhists. In fact, they often feel unfounded vitriol for Israel. In San Jose, I attended an Arab church shortly after getting saved and recall meeting an Arab who identified as an Israeli Christian. Many congregants looked at him with disdain. Their countenance said, "How dare you be here with us?"

This attitude not only worked against how I felt personally but also how I felt biblically. Shortly after my first trip to Israel, I had a dream in which I stood in a desolate land that had clearly been torn apart by war. Buildings were in shambles, and homes were in ruins. I stood there, thinking to myself, *Where am I? Clearly, there has been a war here.* I knew it was the Middle East but was uncertain as to the exact location. Then I saw a large group of people running in one direction to my left. They were running so fast that I couldn't even identify their gender or race! Finally, I had the courage to grab one person's hand to inquire. It was a Jewish woman staring at me in irritation.

"What is going on? Where are we?" I asked.

"We are in Jerusalem and Jesus is coming back," she replied.

She threw off my hand and continued running with her people! I stood in awe. Then I heard the Holy Spirit say to me, "Look! Behind you..." I turned and saw a long line of Saudi people–men, women, and children all lining up behind me so that I couldn't see the end of the line. At that moment, I knew I was leading them to Jerusalem—to the King of Kings, *Jesus!*

While the redemption of my people was an encouraging aspect of the dream, the sign of war was troubling. This prophetic experience came to pass in part in October of

2023, when the Israel/Palestine conflict was heightened yet again. I saw the atrocities committed by Hamas toward the Jewish people (and against Arabs as well, as they will kill anyone if it benefits their agenda). After seeing this, I posted a picture in support of Israel. Many of my Arab Christian friends hated the fact that I did this. To them, it is always about sympathy for the Palestinians and what Israel has done while totally failing to acknowledge Hamas and their provocation. In fact, I was blocked by several people I had known and been friends with for years. This is *imbalanced*.

On the other hand, I saw Western churches in America that were so pro-Israel they did not even acknowledge the suffering of Palestinians and seemed to equate all Palestinian civilians with Hamas—drawing no distinction between the two. They seem to regard Israel as incapable of needing course correction of any kind. When emotions are high, nuance is low. Many in the region and onlookers from abroad fail to view the history and the present situation with an objective eye. Both sides fight over how the conflict started, and they clearly don't see eye to eye over how it will end.

The fact is, the Jewish people settled Israel (then called Canaan), somewhere around the 10th century BC. For centuries upon centuries, the Jewish people suffered exile in places like Babylon and Syria. The Romans destroyed the Second Temple shortly after the time of Christ, and the oppression of the Jews did not get much better after that. After Islam came into being, the Dome of the Rock was built upon the temple ruins in the seventh century, and later, Crusaders massacred Jewish inhabitants en masse. Since establishing their homeland in Israel, most scholars agree that the Jewish people have been kicked out of various nations over 100 times. You only have to look as recently as Germany in World War II to see the irrational, vicious targeting of the Jews.

After centuries of oppression and displacement, the Jews made a move to come back to their homeland in the early 20th century. The narrative that is often sold is that Palestine was an established, unified nation, and the Jewish people showed up in the 1940s to colonize, oppress, and drive out all inhabitants through colonization. In truth, there was no autonomous Palestinian state to colonize. What existed in the region at that time was leftover populations of a Turkish colonial movement that had crumbled. The Middle East had been divided into pieces and given back to various indigenous peoples that had previously been dominated by the Ottoman Empire (which fell around 1922)[20]. After the Ottoman defeat, the League of Nations granted Britain the Mandate for Palestine in 1922, though Britain had already taken control in 1917. The British Mandate officially governed Palestine—including Jerusalem—until 1948, when the State of Israel was established

---

20. One for Israel. "The Origins of the Keffiyeh Headscarf." One for Israel, May 7, 2018. https://www.oneforisrael.org/bible-based-teaching-from-israel/the-origins-of-the-keffiyeh-headscarf/.

on May 14, 1948. Israel became a national state the same day the British departed.

Naturally, Jews for some time had been itching to get back to Jerusalem, and the fall of this power gave them an opportunity to fill the vacuum and reestablish their historical homeland. This provides a different picture of what historical "Palestine" actually is. In fact, one scholar writes, "Before the end of World War I, Palestine formed part of the Ottoman Empire. Under the Ottoman regime, there was no political unit known as Palestine as a political fabrication. Arabs and Jews are cousins, and several Jewish groups even show genetic proximity to Arabs. In fact, the country was better known by its Arab-Muslim name of al-Ard al-Muqadassa | الأرض المقدسة (the Holy Land). Palestine was also referred to as Surya al-Janubiyya | سوريا الجنوبية (Southern Syria), because it was part of geographical Syria, namely the land mass that incorporated present-day Syria, Lebanon, Palestine, and Transjordan."[21]

Historically, Palestine has referred to a region, similar to the Levant or Mesopotamia. It comes from the Greco-Roman Era and was originally called "Palaestina" which was officially applied by the Romans in 135 CE after crushing the Bar Kokhba Revolt, a Jewish uprising against Roman rule. Emperor Hadrian renamed the province from Judea to Syria Palaestina as a way to: Punish the Jews, sever their his-

---

21.   Muhammad Y. Muslih, The Origins of Palestinian Nationalism, (Columbia University Press, 1988) p.11

torical connection to the land, and replace it with a name associated with their historical enemies (the Philistines). The term was used to describe all the inhabitants of the region, regardless of their ethnicity. This included Palestinian Jews and Palestinian Arabs, but there wasn't an ethnically distinct group known as "Palestinians."

As the Jews came back, they wished for a peaceful return to the land that was rightfully theirs. With the backing of the United States, England, and other Western countries, Israel reclaimed their land but not without conflict. We are now approaching 100 years since the return, and the conflict and debate continue, though now it is more inflamed by the religious zeal of Islam. From the start, extremists on the Palestinian side have wanted bloodshed and revenge. Muslims feel as though they are doing a favor for God. Hamas threatens Palestinians that if they leave the Gaza Strip, they will be killed. Meanwhile, they live in palaces in Qatar while waging endless war on the Jews. The Gaza Strip has often been called an "open-air prison." If that's the case, the guards and the warden are the leaders of Hamas who hold the keys.

If Israel put down their weapons, Hamas would kill everyone in Israel and establish a caliphate. If Hamas put down their weapons, peace would come to the land. This is the big difference that no one can deny. The religious fervor of Islamists cannot be overlooked. The thrust of their mentality is vulgar and aims to take territory by force. This was how Saudi Arabia was established—killing Christians and Jews and forcing conversions. It is a fear-based religious machine with terror at the heart. They do not see Israel as a race or a nation but as a tribe worth taking over. Hamas has nothing to do with the historic region of Jerusalem, no more than an Indonesian can lay claim to Canada. Nevertheless, their attacks have been justified and accepted by Muslims and Gentiles who simply fail to understand their motives and history. Hamas will not stop until they've taken every inch of the land. Any time Israel talks about peace and provides a plan, it is thrown out wholesale.

For Muslims, this thinking is inculcated in childhood and remains as they navigate adulthood. Many Arabs fail to see that the Jewish people are a blessing to the region. If they would love them and protect them, the region would flourish. God blesses those who bless Israel (see Genesis 12:3). It is no secret that the United States has prospered, at least in part, because of its support of Israel.

Nevertheless, many remain ignorant on the issue. When the Hamas massacre occurred in October of 2023, I was stunned to see the number of Americans protesting in defense of Hamas and denouncing Israel. The streets were filled with university students who had a loud cry, passion, but little knowledge. Bear in mind, Hamas killed 1,200 people, raped and mutilated women, and took over 250 hostages[22]. Not to mention reports from first responders of a baby found dead in an oven, among other war crimes. Hamas' founding charter itself declares, "The Day of Judgement will not come about until Moslems fight the Jews (killing the Jews), when the Jew will hide behind stones and trees. The stones and trees will say O Moslems, O Abdulla, there is a Jew behind me, come and kill him. Only the Gharkad tree, would not do that because it is one of the trees of the Jews."[23] You are out of your mind if you think what Hamas did is not going to happen in Europe and here in the U.S. They are already here, and our time is coming with Jews first and Christians second; Saturday then Sunday.

Ignorance surrounding Israel and Hamas abounds, which is evidenced by protests at America's top universities like Harvard and Columbia. "From the river to the sea, Palestine will be free," was the mantra on their lips. What river? What sea? Many would likely struggle to answer. It is zeal without knowledge (see Proverbs 19:2). Organizations like *Students for Justice in Palestine* have not only brainwashed young people into antisemitism but, at times, have done the very work of helping sympathy for Hamas take root in the West. It is an infiltration of Western universities by some

---

22. National Center for Biotechnology Information. "Main Body." National Center for Biotechnology Information, U.S. National Library of Medicine, May 10, 2024. https://www.ncbi.nlm.nih.gov/pmc/articles/PMC11010344/#:~:text=Main%20body,crimes%20against%20humanity%20including%20genocide.
23. Hamas Charter, Article 7

of the most heinous leaders on earth. In fact, Haaretz (an Israeli newspaper) found, "based on dozens of conversations with Jewish students on U.S. campuses since October 7, a sizable majority seem to feel that by legitimizing and even glorifying the atrocities perpetrated by Hamas, and by showing no empathy for fellow Jewish students grieving for the victims, SJP has crossed the line from anti-Zionist to antisemitic."[24]

It seems that many in the West have a Palestinian friend showing them biased (propaganda) footage from Al Jazeera, and they base their entire opinion on this alone. I have a friend, for example, who grew up in the Middle East, is now a Christian, and still has hatred for Israel. Her husband is a believer from the U.S., and she said they had never had a fight before this conflict broke out. While she is now starting to see what is going on, it is still an emotionally charged topic.

When the war began in Gaza, Israel gave the Palestinians 21 days to flee because their aim was to attack Hamas, not civilians. Hamas pressured the people to stay. And in their attack, they hit military personnel and civilians alike. You cannot negotiate with terrorists—Hamas must be removed from the face of the earth for any potential peace to occur.

The battle for Israel is happening on multiple fronts.

24. Maltz, Judy (Nov 17, 2023). "What Is Students for Justice in Palestine, the Group Igniting U.S. Campus Wars Over Israel". Haaretz.

Not only is Hamas | حماس out to get Israel, but the Holy Land is continually dealing with Hezbollah | حزب الله, which is headquartered in Lebanon. I was in Lebanon in May of 2023, attending a writing seminar. A connection I had made with a Lebanese publisher led me there, and after the seminar ended, I had three free days. During my travels, I always ask God what is happening in the nation I am visiting and how I should pray while standing on its soil.

One evening, as I prayed on the balcony, I had a vision. I saw Arab believers and Messianic Jews worshiping and singing to God together. Then, suddenly, Hezbollah appeared—an overwhelming darkness. But Israel came against it with force, determined to wipe it from Lebanon. I watched as this black entity was cast into the sea, as though Hezbollah had been erased from existence.

I sat in silence, wondering, *Am I part of this?*

Not long after, I shared the vision with my friend Charlotte. She is Lebanese and her husband is American—both of whom run a gathering of Messianic Jews and Arabs in Cyprus. They had been praying fervently for Lebanon to change, for the country to break free from the grip of Hezbollah. In Lebanon, even saying the name "Israel" is forbidden. During gatherings, she has felt an explosion in the spirit as Arabs pray over Jews and Jews pray over Arabs.

Months after sharing these things, I met for a prayer meeting with believers from Muslim backgrounds and Messianic Jewish sisters, where we connected, encouraged one another, and prayed for Israel. During the meeting, Lebanon launched an attack on Israel. Here we were, coming together to seek unity in the Middle East between Jews and Arabs, yet war was breaking out. We read Psalm 91 and prayed together fervently.

Not long after, the news broke—Hezbollah's leader had been killed. On September 27, 2024, in Beirut, Israel launched a strike that killed Hassan Nasrallah, the longtime Secretary-General of Lebanese Hezbollah.

Charlotte sent me a message: "Your vision came true."

I rejoiced. The destroyer had been destroyed.

Lebanon is a nation of brilliant, educated people, but Hezbollah has held them in oppression for years. It was once called the "West of the Middle East," a place of culture, prosperity, and freedom. But Hezbollah changed everything, taking control of the government, airports, economic policy, and more. Everything fell into ruin under their grip.

And now, the leader and his team were gone.

There is always a time given to repent. My family, like many in the Arab world, was furious with Israel. But I couldn't share in their grief. Instead, *I danced.*

* * *

In early 2024, I encountered a man named Mosab Hassan Yousef who had authored a book entitled *Son of Hamas.* In discovering more, I felt my eyes begin to open in new ways. I strongly recommend everyone read his book, not just because of his insight into the situation in the Middle East, but because of Yousef's unique *experience*. He is the son of the founder of Hamas. Many years ago, Israel offered him to work as a spy within Hamas, feeding information to Israeli intelligence in order to thwart terrorist attacks. He left Islam, became a Christian, and lived to tell his story as a leader within Hamas, and he is now an outspoken and qualified voice on the issue. In 2007, he quit his work as a spy and led a quiet life on an island in South Asia. After the October 7th attacks, he came back into the public eye and has not been silent since. He is a man on a mission. As someone who has worked within both Hamas and the Israeli military, he is perhaps the most qualified person on earth to speak on the issue. I highly recommend his interviews as further resources on the topic.

How should a Westerner respond to all of this? To put it simply: be educated, be objective, and be prayerful. If the situation matters to God, it should matter to us. Support Israel and pray for her peace. At the same time, separate Hamas from civilian Palestinians. In the midst of my renouncing Islam and Hamas, I want to make it very clear that I pray for and advocate for the civilians in Palestine to experience a prosperous and safe future.

Before the attacks, a video came out of the Crown Prince of Saudi Arabia, Mohammed bin Salman (MBS), in which he discussed peace with Israel. He put his money where his mouth was, even hiring an Israeli company to manage certain aspects of IT in Saudi—an unprecedented act of goodwill. This, of course, angered many Saudis. After the attacks, he advocated for the plight of Palestinians, and left it at that—not speaking against Israel as many in the past would have.

My prayer is that MBS and the current Saudi administration would act to help Palestinian civilians. This means building good schools, offering passports, and giving them an umbrella to live under in the rich land of Saudi Arabia. Spiritually speaking, I believe the land belongs to the Jewish people. Palestine is better off having the Jewish people rule over it. We have evidence that this works. Arabs are thriving in Israel, and they are not fans of the Palestinian state. The UN gave money for Palestinian aid, but of course, this all goes to enrich Hamas—not the people. The only hope for Palestinian civilians is to remove Hamas and offer opportunity elsewhere while the Gaza Strip is rebuilt.

Westerners must be watchful and critical in their research. The antisemitic propaganda is strong. Hamas is backed with the covering of Qatar and money from Iran as well. They are all united in hatred for Israel to the point that the Sunni and Shia divide doesn't even matter, so long as money is spent to wipe out the Jews. In fact, after the attacks happened, Al Jazeera went so far as to show footage from when ISIS invaded Syria and told the public that this was what Israel was doing in the Gaza Strip.

As with any war waged by tyrants, propaganda is strongly at play. Exercise caution with the mainstream media, as you may wind up more confused than before you started. Be a self-starter and an independent learner. Look for independent journalists on the ground who are providing firsthand accounts. Find those who understand both sides and avoid secondhand information. I haven't come to these conclusions from one news clipping or a singular voice. I might be a slow adopter and take time to reach conclusions, but once I do, I am immovable, not in the cause of man, but in the cause of God.

The truth is, both Muslims and Jews reject the fact that Jesus is the Son of God. Both parties have a veil over their eyes, preventing them from seeing Jesus for who He truly is. As a believer from a Mulsim background, knowing the truth about who Jesus is comes with a huge responsibility to share with both Muslims and Jews alike. Some Christians stand with Palestinians, thinking God is punishing Israel for their rebellion—using Hamas to do so. Others think they are being nice by refusing to take a side. The question becomes, if God is taking a side (and He is), *why don't we?*

As followers of Jesus, regardless of our backgrounds, we know Him intimately, we know His words, we know what the Bible teaches, and we should be the ones who share the biblical knowledge and the truth we have with our brothers and sisters about who the Jewish people are and the significance of Israel. Just as Joseph's brothers cried when he revealed to them who he was—their Jewish brother—Jewish people will mourn as for an only son and grieve bitterly for him, as one grieves for a firstborn (see Zechariah 12:10). Jesus weeps with His brothers and sisters as well.

It is so hard for some Christians to take a side in this conflict. They know that God is love, but because of that, they feel He is only nice, and they lose sight of Him as Judge and Warrior. It is not as though God was Judge in the Old Testament (The Hebrew Bible) and now has magically become a sweet, kind pushover. He has not changed; He is who He is. He was and is and always will be the same.

The Lord goes out like a mighty man,
like a man of war he stirs up his zeal;
he cries out, he shouts aloud,
he shows himself mighty against his foes.
For a long time I have held my peace;
I have kept still and restrained myself;
now I will cry out like a woman in labor;
I will gasp and pant. (Isaiah 42:13-14)

There are people who won't talk to me anymore over this issue, yet I am standing on principle. I know believers who have expressed anger toward God over the issue and are losing sleep and weight due to restlessness and fatigue. To Muslims who begin following Jesus, leaving their faith was already a huge slap in the face to their families. Siding with Israel on a geopolitical issue is like betraying them afresh, and to some, it is simply not worth the cost.

During that fateful fall of 2023, it was crushing to see what was happening in the land I had visited and loved less than a year before. The situation only served to heighten my love and compassion for those in the region. How my calling works out there does not fall on my shoulders, but God will order it properly. After the first trip to Israel, I had many dreams. Piece by piece, God has been revealing things to me. While I do not have the full picture, I know that I will reside in Israel at some point, even if for a season. The story of God is one of love and the multiplication of truth. *This* combination will bring heaven to earth, just as it brought heaven to earth in the days of Jesus' ministry on earth. As I move ahead in my calling, I fully intend to reproduce the same pattern both here and abroad.

CHAPTER THIRTEEN

The Return

My Heart Forever Tethered in Jerusalem, 2024

"The place God calls you to is the place where your deep gladness and the world's deep hunger meet."

—FREDERICK BUECHNER

Returning to Israel after the attacks, I wondered if there would be heightened security and scrutiny upon entry. I was pulled aside at customs, which was to be expected, and taken to the office of a sweet lady who had many, many questions, all of which I answered politely with a smile. We talked for an hour and a half, where I discussed my organization as she took ample notes.

At the end of the questioning, she said, "Thank you for what you do—keep doing what you're doing," and handed me my passport. It was a welcome bit of encouragement from an unexpected source. Sure, it was a longer entry process than the first trip, but I felt just as "at home" as ever as

I made my way past the gates and into the fresh, sunny air of the Holy Land.

While I focused my first trip around Nazareth and certain key organizations, I planned my return trip as more of a research project. I spent the first three days in Tel Aviv, relaxing on the beach, praying, walking, and journaling. From there, I passed the remaining nine days in Jerusalem.

As I checked in at the hotel in Jerusalem, the front desk worker was surprised to see a booking from a foreigner. As you might imagine, the war had greatly reduced tourism in the region. He thought I was Hispanic and then guessed I was a Sephardic Jew from North Africa. He was surprised to see that the birthplace listed on my passport was Saudi Arabia, and even more surprised to find out I was a Christian—just like him.

He wound up being a great help during my trip, providing local knowledge and directions as needed. We sat down to have coffee at the hotel and talked for some time. I learned that he had a Greek mother and a father who lived locally in Jerusalem, he had previously lived in Germany, and he was fluent in five languages. Whether I needed to know where to get a coffee or how to attend a Shabbat dinner, he had the insight I needed. As he took me to my room, he noted the view from my window, which was the main government building. "Maybe this is a good spot for you to stand and pray for our country," he said.

I passed my days sightseeing, visiting monuments, museums, and praying quietly. I walked through the ornate stone buildings of the Jewish quarter and navigated the narrow alleys leading to yeshivas[25] and synagogues. I admit I felt a little out of place at times. I went to the Wailing Wall, which was a powerful experience in itself. I heard voices of worship in beautiful native languages that felt like both a prayer gathering and a celebration. I wrote heartfelt prayers on a note and placed them in the designated slots in the wall[26].

After a few days, I moved to a hotel in the city center. The city center was lively with music, shops, cafes, and restaurants all bustling with activity in and around Zion Square. From morning to night, it seemed that no one ever went home and that everyone in the city was out and about. This changed, however, on Friday nights. Shabbat was shut down, unlike anything I have experienced before. From Friday to Saturday, the entire city was asleep, so to speak, with families all staying home faithfully adhering to the practice which has persisted for thousands of years.

It felt so strange in the city. No one was outside as I went out to walk alone. I so appreciated the tradition, the values, and the Jewish observance of festivals. As a person with a Saudi background, you would think I would feel at home

---

25. A traditional Jewish educational institution focused on the study of Rabbinic literature.
26. For over 200 years, people have written prayer notes on paper and placed them in the cracks in the wall. Over 1 million prayer notes are placed each year.

amongst Muslims or former Muslims. As a person living in the West, you would think I would feel at home in American society. Yet only God can suspend my logic and make me feel at home amongst Messianic Jews, which He has done supernaturally.

One of the great joys of the trip was attending a Shabbat dinner | תבש תודועס with a family in Jerusalem. They had candles on the table, a feast of delicious food, and braided bread | הלח. They started with praising God, saying, "Blessed are You, Lord our God, King of the universe, who has brought forth bread from the earth," and they ended the meal with a blessing as well.

It was a sweet and special time—a Middle Eastern dinner and family gathering wrapped in the grace and love of Jesus. The husband blessed his wife by reading from Proverbs 31 (a woman of valor | אשת חיל) and honored her in front of her children. The kids then stood up and recited, "Her children rise up and call her blessed" (Proverbs 31:28). The father blessed me as a daughter alongside the children. I felt cherished, honored, and I thought to myself, *This feels like home, a redeemed Middle Eastern culture by the blood of the Lamb! This is how it should be: everything is rooted and anchored in the love of the Father for us.*

They sang worship songs in Hebrew, and their voices and singing brought tears to my eyes as I envisioned my siblings one day gathering at a Shabbat dinner, worshiping Jesus, giving honor, and singing praises to our Father in heaven, where we all know we are not fatherless anymore. Our heavenly Father is in our midst, and His Holy Spirit makes us one in Him. Together we sang the Shabbat shalom song known as Shalom Aleichem | שלום עליכם, literally, *peace be upon you.* It was a capstone experience during this glorious return trip.

My calling to Israel | ישראל has become the highest mandate, even causing me to lose friends. It grieves me to say, once again, that I've lost some dear Palestinian friends and some Arabs who are supporters of the Palestinian cause. What else is there to lose? I've already lost my life, only to find it.

I've chosen to walk the narrow path, to press in, and if that means losing all, so be it—I know His goodness and mercy will follow me all the days of my life. I have a personal history with God, a record of meetings with Him in the secret place where He has spoken precious things and given prophetic guidance that is more real than the very room I sit in. I have seen Him open doors that no man can shut, so why fear? He is unfolding a strategic plan for my life to be in Jerusalem | ירושלים, where the governmental capital of the world will be, as King Jesus returns to rule forever and ever.

But my story and connection to this region are not the only ones that God is writing. Across the region, He's moving in ways that only He can. One of the most surprising and beautiful confirmations of this came in the night seasons. In fact, I'd like to share a dream that one of my Jewish sisters in the Messiah had—a woman named Talya, who lives in Israel. This dream came to her months before we ever met. When she later heard my story, she knew I was the woman from her dream. I share it here, in her own words, as a testimony of how the Lord speaks across cultures, borders, and even in our sleep.

A few months before meeting Sahar, I had a vivid dream that I recorded afterward. In the dream, my friend Sarah came to meet me, and suddenly, we found ourselves in a large convention-style room, like one you'd see in a hotel. The room was filled with people from all over the world and across time—leaders, historical figures, and others significant in the history of Israel and the Middle East. Sarah and I stood to the side, watching as plaques and photographs were displayed, honoring these individuals for their contributions to Israel.

Then I noticed one plaque that stood out. Unlike the others, it had no photograph—just a name. I recognized the name as belonging to one of my Moroccan relatives, but the absence of a picture intrigued me.

As the scene unfolded, the atmosphere suddenly changed. Jesus and His twelve disciples entered the room and walked through it with purpose. Before they appeared, the room had been full of chatter and political discussions. But the moment they entered, everything shifted. People began following them as they moved from the front of the room to a double door at the back that led to another room, almost like a banquet hall. At that moment, it was as though the political arguments and noise melted away, and I knew that Jesus was going to make all truth known.

Near the door where Jesus and His disciples exited, there was a round table. Sitting there was a woman completely covered, like the traditional black garments worn by women in Saudi Arabia. As she was eating some of the treats that were being offered at the gathering, she began to cry. Sarah and I noticed her and felt drawn to her. At that moment, someone stated that she was the person from the missing photograph on the plaque. Then we understood why her photo was missing from the plaque: She was a Jewish woman from Saudi Arabia—a member of a strict tribe that didn't allow photographs and didn't allow themselves to enjoy even simple pleasures, like tasty food. She was crying because she had just tasted the food and couldn't believe how good it was.

As we looked at her, she turned to me and started to cry and cry, saying, "I can't believe I missed Him," speaking of Jesus. I gave her a hug and started crying with her, and I gently responded, "You didn't...you didn't!" I knew we could just go into the next room and see Him, and she knew He was the Messiah. I began sharing with her about all of the awesome wonders of the Kingdom of Heaven, and how we will sit with Yeshua and learn of all of His greatness. Then I woke up.

Several weeks after having this dream, I met with Sarah and told her about it. What's incredible is that I had little to no prior connection or knowledge of Saudi Arabia, but I knew this dream was significant enough to share it with Sarah. She was amazed as she told me about a Saudi Arabian Christian woman she had just met who had come to Israel and shared her testimony. That woman was Sahar. Through a series of events divinely orchestrated by the Lord, I finally met Sahar, and I was stunned. She was the woman from my dream. After getting to know her testimony and background, I understood that God was using her to bridge the gaps between cultures and faiths in the Middle East.

* * *

Before Daniel in the Old Testament (The Hebrew Bible) had influence for God in Babylon, he had to become familiar with the "language and the literature" of the Chaldeans (see Daniel 1:4). In other words, he was educated in the region where he was serving. For people who are mission-minded, it's not just about knowing the Bible but knowing the place and the people. This particular trip to Israel for me was a chance to immerse myself in the history of the region and better grasp the people and the times.

I learned of Israel's progress since re-establishing its homeland less than 100 years ago. I saw the rough desert they started with and looked around to appreciate the rich oasis that was now established. As I walked into the ANU Museum of the Jewish People in Tel Aviv, a flood of soldiers happened to enter with me. I heard their stories and saw their perspectives firsthand. I spoke with one of the soldiers for a moment, and he described feeling a sense of duty, wanting to bring victory over evil—not just to Israel but to the world. I had the sense that I was talking to an older brother. In a sense, Israel is the older brother of the free world, and he continues to make sacrifices on our behalf.

Later in the trip, as I navigated another museum called the Museum of Tolerance in Jerusalem, I came into the new exhibit called *Journey into the Heart,* which highlighted the October 7th attacks. On a wall by itself was a note that one of the Islamic attackers had in his pocket at the time of his death. The note itself was in Farsi and said, "You must sharpen the blades of your sword before Allah. Know that the enemy is a disease and has no cure. Attack them." I was disturbed but not surprised in the least. The battle against the evils of Islam is real and spiritual.

I've watched many testimonies of survivors from the October attacks who shared their experiences. One woman hid in a trash can to escape gunfire and explosions. After realizing it was not the best shelter, she left to find cover from missile strikes and was shot in the hip and crippled. Other people are still searching for missing family members.

Lately in prayer, God has referred to me as *Ranger* and has wrapped His words to me in military-type language. I discovered that an airborne ranger is able to endure the hardest of conditions; they are a sort of military first responder, and when dispatched, can be anywhere in the world in less than eight hours, ready to carry out the mission. God took me to Judges 6, where I read about the life of Gideon and saw that the Lord was calling me to a warrior status as well. While it would be nice to dwell in peaceful settings with no turmoil, I cannot escape the fact that God has called me as a spiritual ranger to map territory and stand in battle against the principalities and powers that rule the air.

Those who dwell in Israel are no strangers to battle. Everywhere I went, I met people who lived with a keen awareness of the brutal history and the brutal current events happening in the land. Even while getting my hair done, the stylist was a Sephardic Jew who I noticed had a brace on his foot. He came to Israel to train to fight, and during battle, he was shot in the foot by Hamas.

"We are glad you're here," he said. "You love the Jewish people."

I met another lady who was gearing up for boot camp to join the fight as well. Beyond these chance meetings, I visited a church and attended a ministry meeting where a leader invited me to hear a live recording of their session on government. It was a chance to learn even more, and I did not pass that up.

I've noticed a trend as of late in Israel, which is a sort of homecoming. On one occasion during the trip, I left my bag next to the lounge chair I was sitting on at the beach. I had gotten up, and when I came back, a lady had taken my spot. I quietly grabbed my bag and intended to find a new spot when she realized her error and apologized.

"Sit, sit," she said. "I like your energy. Are you Arab, maybe?"

We talked and I learned that she was originally an Algerian Jew raised in France. Because of the conflict at hand, she was in the process of moving to Israel and learning Hebrew. Waves of people from around the world are coming back to the historic homeland. Believers around the world must open their eyes to see the fulfillment of prophecy playing out before their very eyes! God used Jewish people to bring Jesus to the world 2,000 years ago, and He will use them again to bring Him back! "For I tell you, you will **not** see me again, until you say, 'Blessed is he who comes in the name of the Lord'" (Matthew 23:39).

As my trip came to a close, I felt the Lord telling me to spend the last three days at the Waldorf Astoria hotel. I was reluctant at first, given the price of a room, but complied. Per usual, I quickly found out why God spoke this. The annual Jerusalem prayer breakfast was being hosted in that very hotel while I was there, and I was delighted to meet new people, forge fresh connections, and continue to see the plan of God transition from mere blueprints to reality. While I don't have the complete picture for my calling in Israel, I know those pieces will come together. In fact, I believe these missing puzzle pieces are locked in people that I'll meet by divine appointment. There is a timed release of these puzzle pieces, and only God can lead me to them. I am trusting Him to do so as He has many times in the past.

While my time in Israel has been overwhelmingly smooth, it is not without difficulty. On this particular trip, I had some trouble during my departure after arriving at the airport. I was quickly pulled aside and brought into a room where I was made to stand for three hours while being interrogated. "Can I use the bathroom?" I asked a couple of hours into the questioning.

"No," I was told.

Nevertheless, I continued smiling and answering peacefully, which was met with eye-rolling from my interrogator. I simply answered the questions and was an open book with my goals, intentions, and organization. After that, another lady who was quite apologetic frisked me. From there, they confiscated my bags, laptop, and told me they would ship them to my destination—which they did. After the ordeal, a man rushed me straight to the plane, as I almost missed my flight home. I boarded with just my phone in hand.

I would much rather be questioned by Israeli authorities than Saudi authorities, and in part, I am almost glad that it happened. Now I am known to them, and my clear intention of serving and blessing the region is on record with them.

Because of what God is showing me in the spiritual and the natural, the dreams, the open visions, and the prophetic words, I believe my calling is bigger than I currently realize. I truly believe the Lord is giving me a spiritual authority as well as governmental authority. What He is calling me to will require an anointing similar to that of Joseph, Deborah, Gideon, or Esther. I must carry a fierce warrior-like spirit with a zeal for truth and justice, while maintaining the meek heart of a true servant. In my identity in the flesh, I am a descendant of the Arabic people, but in my identity in the Spirit, I am a daughter of God. Just like Moses, I refused to join the Arabic people in their sin against Israel and chose to suffer mistreatment along with the people of God (see Hebrews 11:24). After all, I have been grafted into the Olive Tree, which represents Israel.

Before, during, and after my trips to Israel, the fire for that region has burned and will continue to burn within me. Dreams have unfolded, and visions have been given.

Insight is continuing to come my way, and plans are being firmed up. During one dream in particular, I was with someone, laughing and talking. Suddenly, I felt a pain in my belly. The scene cut, and I was in a doctor's office. The doctor looked at me and said, "I have good news for you, you are pregnant...with twins."

Confused, I prayed, and the Lord responded, "You have two nations in your womb, Sahar."

"Who are they?" I asked.

"Arabs and Jews."

My calling was even more solidified at that moment.

I saw a biblical picture of God's invitation to the Middle East found in Isaiah, "Arise, shine, for your light has come, and the glory of the Lord has risen upon you" (Isaiah 60:1). The prodigals and deniers throughout the Middle East will find their way to Zion[27], they will seek their way to the Son. The chapter goes on to describe, "...the sons of foreigners shall build up your walls" (verse 10). Three cities mentioned in this area of Scripture (Midian, Ephah, and Kedar) are all within Saudi Arabia. I personally believe the wealth in Saudi will play a part in the rebuilding of Jerusalem for the return of the King: "Then you shall see and become radiant, and your heart shall swell with joy; Because the abundance of the sea shall be turned to you, the wealth of the Gentiles shall come to you" (Isaiah 60:5). God's timeline is perfectly orchestrated, calculated, unmoving, and certain.

---

27. "...whose heart are the highways to Zion" (Psalm 84:5).

I saw and heard surprises, new ideas, possibilities, and a future with God and His purposes. Up to now, my life has not been a predictable path. My steps have been ordered by the Lord, which often means you don't know what your next step is at all. Nevertheless, I would rather live with the risk of trusting God than in the false security of man's blueprints. Anything precious is worth fighting for, and I believe the regions of the Middle East are worth a fierce and glorious fight. In the words of the Psalmist, "Gird your sword on your thigh, O mighty one, in your splendor and majesty! In your majesty ride out victoriously for the cause of truth and meekness and righteousness; let your right hand teach you awesome deeds! Your arrows are sharp in the heart of the king's enemies; the peoples fall under you. Your throne, O God, is forever and ever. The scepter of your kingdom is a scepter of uprightness" (Psalm 45:3-6).

You Are Invited

Find your sister

Every year on July 22nd, I clear a day on my schedule to do nothing but spend time with the Lord. I put off errands, phone calls, task lists, meetings, and ministry to simply be with Him. This particular day marks my spiritual birthday—the anniversary of my salvation. It's a time of sweet worship, prayer, and reflection when I think back to when the veil from my eyes was removed and I could truly begin to *see.*

It is impossible for me to sit aside and enjoy the benefits of salvation without burning to extend this invitation to the world as well. May I implore you, ladies, *invite your sisters!* May I implore you, men, *invite your brothers!* So many are yearning for something more, but are without a plausible alternative. Like I did, they are questioning the dogma of their youth and crying out for a newfound freedom. *You* can be God's delivery system of hope and freedom through Jesus. Go beyond praying a prayer and truly learn to lead. Whether it's combining faith and fashion or leading a small group or donating to missions, take the step to be part of God's invitation to the world.

Some of those I have discipled over the years have made extraordinary progress and have remarkable testimonies of their own. Others fall by the wayside and see no transformation. For the people who experience change, they are humble, teachable, and want God for more than what He can do for them. Others are unwilling to pay the price of change and let go of old ideas. As a result, the door remains shut, and they are *happily stuck*. Nevertheless, the invitation remains the same: Let Jesus have His way.

Is there a price to pay? Of course. Good things always require sacrifice and the calling of God is no exception. What I have had to lay down in terms of my family relationships has been immense, but worthwhile. I recall being in the presence of God on one occasion in an inner healing session. I saw myself sitting with Jesus, and I said, "I'm tired, God. The journey is not easy. I feel like giving up."

He lovingly responded, "The cross was hard, Sahar. I didn't want to go there! But I did it for you, I brought the victory for all of you. You might suffer a little now, but the reward is big and resurrection is coming. What I have for you is BIG, BIG, BIG." Then He showed me the faces of people, masses of people, who were waiting for me. Whether it's ministry, dating, programs, hobbies, or personal pursuits, I am mission-focused, and my life revolves around this call of God on my life.

I simply don't have time to waste wandering about in the wilderness. Daily, I operate with an extreme sense of focus for what lies ahead. Usually, after a slow morning of time with the Lord, I read and allow God to provide ideas. Ideation is one of my top strengths, and as concepts pop up, I look for grace upon them. From that place of prayer and ideation, I set out to work, generally until about 10 pm daily—the lines between private life and ministry are often blurred. Translation projects, screenplays, meetings, fund-raising, planning trips, and raising up leaders are just a few of the standard tasks at hand.

After Nabeel passed, I attended the funeral, which was full of attendees who were both grieving the loss and celebrating the life. Until then, I had never seen a dead person, yet there he was in the open casket, wearing his favorite shirt, looking peaceful. *He is so young,* I thought, *just a year older than me, but his life was so fruitful.* I said a quiet prayer and heard the Spirit respond, "I'm going to use you through media. I made you to stand out, and when you do, nations will be free."

"My mom will be so ashamed of me," I said. "She already hates me and won't talk to me."

Jesus said, "Who gives you honor, Sahar?"

"You do, Lord."

"Then why are you worried about your mom shaming you?"

"Ok, God, I'll do it."

Since then, a digital mini-series has been created, and more acting opportunities are on the horizon—all to shed light on the Muslim experience in America and ultimately to lift up the name of Jesus. The director of the series was gracious as I played the role of Zahra, a Saudi newcomer to the States. As I donned the hijab for the role, it was emotionally overwhelming as I looked back at how far God had brought me, and as I realized how many women are still there.

I want all that we do in ministry, the projects, the media, the teaching, to provide a message of hope to women in the Middle East. Many care deeply about peace building between Arabs and Jews, but have not been given the courage to do something about it. May we inspire and influence women to connect, love one another, and develop a brighter future for the Middle East. I believe women have a great calling to rise up to serve their societies, governments, and nations. The modern-day Esthers, Deborahs, Marys, and Jochebeds are rising in power!

* * *

Since getting saved and starting a ministry, I have gained a community, lost some, and lost some more. This may just be the reality for me as I navigate my calling in the most divided regions of the world. I have overcome pushback for being a woman in ministry and have defied the borders and constraints of life for the usual Saudi woman. Yet I cannot help but feel the wind of a loving, fierce God in my sails. He is a warrior and defender.

Yes, God is loving and good, but we cannot separate His loving tenderness from His fierce protection. It brings to mind a story from my childhood. Growing up, we had cats in the house and around the neighborhood. One cute little white cat really captured my heart and became my tiny companion.

One day, a boy in the neighborhood stole my cat, and I was absolutely devastated. It felt like my own little child being torn from my arms. I could do nothing. Fortunately, I had a plan. As the door opened and my father came into the house from work, I cried, fell into his arms, and told him what had happened. Without pause, without hesitation, he responded, "Show me the house."

We drove through the neighborhood, and I pointed to the home where the boy lived. Exiting the car, I stood by his side as we approached the front door. My father knocked, and the boy answered, holding the cat. "Is this your cat?" he asked the boy with a voice so stern, serious, and probably scary if you were on the receiving end of the question.

"No," the boy said.

"Then give it back to her. Now."

I stood next to my dad, smiling, so joyous and proud as the cat was given back to me. We walked back to the car, and a warm feeling filled my chest. I was defended, cared for, and honored by a fierce, passionate father who knew what was best for his girl. In the years ahead, when my earthly father would not be around to ensure that what was stolen was returned to me, my heavenly Father would walk by my side to get back everything that the enemy stole. He would act to restore my honor, to reinstate my purpose, to dismiss the lies, and to *unveil beauty*.

What Now?

How to Get Involved

Our vision is expanding, and I am stepping into a season of transformation. What started as *Unveiling Beauty*—a courageous sisterhood of women from around the world who have left Islam to follow Jesus—has now evolved into something even greater. United by faith and love, we've walked this incredible journey together, finding freedom, healing, and a deeper sense of purpose in Him.

This journey has led me to dream of launching projects that prompt the bringing together of both men and women—Arabs and Jews—who are committed to fostering unity, understanding, and collaboration. God is leading me to diplomacy and making peace through acceptance and dialogue. Having faced persecution for our faith and identity, we share a profound desire for a future where we can live freely in the Middle East—a future where peace, love, and religious freedom aren't just ideals, but tangible realities.

Through meaningful dialogue, collaborative initiatives, and community-driven projects, I'm going beyond personal transformation and actively working to break down barriers, build bridges, and cultivate mutual respect. My mission is no longer just about my journey; it's about creating a lasting legacy of peace—one where Arabs and Jews join forces to shape a future rooted in coexistence, dignity, and hope.

This is more than a vision, it's a call to action, and a powerful movement of reconciliation. We are committed to building a world where diversity is celebrated and peace is not just a dream, but a reality. I'm seeking to connect and collaborate with like-minded individuals, organizations, and synagogues who share this vision—to speak, to connect, and to bring people together in ways that transform hearts and communities.

Christians, though a small minority in the land of Israel, have often remained silent, shaped by replacement theology, which strips God's covenant from the Jewish people.

But a new voice is rising.

Followers of Christ from Muslim backgrounds are stepping into the gap, not timid, not silenced, but fierce with love, bold in truth, and full of compassion for both peoples. We carry a prophetic call to heal what history has broken and to proclaim that the God of Abraham has not abandoned His people. His covenant still stands. His promises still breathe through Romans 11 and 12.

I know deep in my spirit—and history affirms—that some of us carry Jewish heritage in our very blood and DNA. When Islam expanded, it conquered vast lands and many people groups. In the process, countless Jews fled. Others were forced to convert. But their stories didn't vanish—they became woven into our roots.

Early Islamic history makes this clear. The Hadith and early records mention Jewish tribes that lived and thrived in Arabia: Banu Khaybar (قبيلة بني خيبر), Banu Nadir (بنو النضير), Banu Qurayza (بنو قريظة), Banu Qaynuqa (بنو قينقاع), Banu Tha'laba (بنو ثعلبة), Banu Awf (بنو عوف), Banu Hudhayl (بنو هدل), and Banu 'Ikrimah (بنو عكرمة).

To think that some of us—Arabs, Saudis, and those raised in Islamic traditions—may carry the blood of these ancient Jewish tribes...To realize that the people we were taught to distrust, even hate, might in fact be our own relatives—our people.

These Jewish tribes lived, traded, and flourished in the heart of Arabia long before Islamic conquest. Many vanished from the pages of history. But blood remembers what history forgets.

If Christians from Christian backgrounds remain blind or bound by silence, we former Muslims who now follow Yeshua...

We will rise.

We will be the bridge.

We will bring peace.

I am sure of this and I see it because the Jewish Messiah, Yeshua, didn't just save us. He realigned us with the ancient story—the story of Abraham, Isaac, and Jacob. He brought us home to the God of Israel. And in that homecoming, our hearts began to beat in rhythm with His heart for His people.

CURRENT FILM PROJECT OF TAJ62

A transformative story of a young Saudi woman in LA who encounters Jesus and must confront her past, family, and identity. Reemas bridges East & West, Shia & Sunni, Arab & Jew.

VISION AND SYNOPSIS

Reemas, a devout Saudi Muslim, lands in Los Angeles, ready to chase her dream of becoming a fashion designer. But the city of endless possibilities quickly becomes the backdrop for an even bigger journey—one that will turn her world upside down.

In LA, Reemas encounters Daliah, a strong-willed Palestinian real estate agent and passionate follower of Jesus. Her story is unlike anything Reemas has ever heard, and it sets off a chain of events that challenges everything she's known about faith, family, and identity. As she's introduced to a hidden world of believers from across the Arab world, Reemas begins to question everything. But things get even more complicated when she meets Vered, a Jewish business owner, whose perspective on Israel ignites a fiery conflict with Daliah—throwing Reemas into a whirlwind of questions about history, faith, and identity.

And just when Reemas thinks things couldn't get more intense, she falls head over heels for a charming Kuwaiti man. But their love story is no fairytale—his Sunni background and her Shia heritage throw them into a passionate and painful clash of cultures, adding fuel to an already explosive journey. Meanwhile, her mother's relentless pressure to finish school and return home to marry only adds to the chaos, leaving Reemas torn between two worlds.

Amid love, betrayal, faith, and fierce self-discovery, Reemas embarks on a path that leads her to an unexpected destination—Jesus, baptism, and the courage to live out her transformation in a world that doesn't always understand her.

The film will be 85-95% in Arabic. It is written by and designed specifically for Khaleeji (Arabian Gulf) women and families, but there will be a broad appeal across the Arabic-speaking world.

The film will be 90-120 minutes long, designed first to

be played on Global Netflix and on as many other digital and traditional film and television platforms as possible.

THE OPPORTUNITY AND NEED

The Kingdom of Saudi Arabia (KSA), the Gulf, and the broader Muslim world are experiencing profound change, both socially and spiritually.

From a media perspective, Saudi Arabia is undergoing a cultural shift. The country now has movie theaters, and indigenous filmmakers and artists are stepping up to produce more diverse and compelling content. Many Saudis are using VPNs to access content from international platforms, further shaping the media landscape. Socially, KSA has seen groundbreaking changes: women have been driving for the past seven years, female guardianship laws have been eliminated, and progressive business initiatives are being championed by the Crown Prince.

Spiritually, there's a rising tide of curiosity and faith, with many reports showing an increasing number of spiritual seekers and Christ followers in Saudi Arabia.

Based on our field research and conversations with industry professionals across the Middle East, it's clear that the time is ripe for high-quality, Kingdom-driven media content—not only for Saudi Arabia but for the entire region.

The story of *Reemas* is especially timely and compelling. It speaks directly to the hearts and minds of Saudi women, many of whom have lived under societal constraints and are now experiencing newfound freedoms. As Saudi society undergoes such dramatic changes, it has stirred a deeper interest in spirituality, leading many to explore faith in ways they never have before.

Sahar is happy to discuss the project further if you feel compelled to partner with her in this endeavor. She welcomes the opportunity to collaborate with individuals or organizations who share the vision and passion for bringing this transformative story to life.

For More information, visit:

www.UnveilingBeauty.org

To join our Jews/Arabs peacebuilding network,
please email us at:

Sahar@RisingTogether.network

To partner with us about the Film Project,
please reach us at:

Sahar@Taj62.media

A Personal Note from the Author

This is only the beginning.

What you've just read isn't just my story—it's a glimpse into a journey that's still unfolding. And if something in these pages stirred your heart...then maybe, just maybe, we're meant to keep walking together.

I've created a space just for you—a blog where you'll find stories, sisterhood, peacemaking between Arabs and Jews, and Spirit-led reflections. It's a sacred place, and I'd be deeply honored to have you join me there.

There is still so much to be unveiled. And you're invited.

Join the community of sisterhood—where we can chat, share ideas, and encourage one another as we walk with Jesus, together.

Visit me at:

wwwBySahar.blog

Follow the journey. Share your story. Walk unveiled.

Thus says the LORD:

"Stand in the roads and look. Ask for the ancient paths where the good way דֶּרֶךְ *is—and* **walk in it.** *Then you will find rest for your souls. But they said, 'We won't walk in it.'"*

JEREMIAH 6:16

About the Author

Sahar Saeed | סהר סעיד | سهر سعيد is a Saudi-American voice of truth, transformation, and reconciliation. Raised in a devout Shia Muslim family, her worldview was radically reshaped by a life-changing encounter with Yeshua—an awakening that shattered inherited narratives and ignited a calling to unite Arabs and Jews. Today, she is a writer, speaker, and fierce advocate for peace, healing, and mutual understanding across historic divides. Sahar is currently pursuing her M.A. in Government: International Relations and Human Rights at Liberty University, equipping herself to serve as both a diplomatic and prophetic voice in the Middle East. Once taught to fear Jews and reject Israel, she now stands boldly as a bridge-builder between former enemies—declaring a new story of hope, shared destiny, and Kingdom purpose. And she's just getting started.